# Redistricting and Representation

Pundits have observed that if so many incumbents are returned to Congress each election by such wide margins, perhaps we should look for ways to increase competitiveness—a centerpiece to the American way of life—through redistricting. Do competitive elections increase voter satisfaction? How does voting for a losing candidate affect voters' attitudes toward government? The not-so-surprising conclusion is that losing voters are less satisfied with Congress and their Representative, but the implications for the way in which we draw congressional and state legislative districts are less straightforward.

*Redistricting and Representation* argues that competition in general elections is not the sine qua non of healthy democracy, and that it in fact contributes to the low levels of approval of Congress and its members. Brunell makes the case for a radical departure from traditional approaches to redistricting—arguing that we need to "pack" districts with as many like-minded partisans as possible, maximizing the number of winning voters, not losers.

**Thomas L. Brunell** is Associate Professor of Political Science at the University of Texas at Dallas.

Part of the **Controversies in Electoral Democracy and Representation** Series edited by Matthew J. Streb.

## Controversies in electoral democracy and representation
Series Editor: Matthew J. Streb

The Routledge series *Controversies in Electoral Democracy and Representation* presents cutting-edge scholarship and innovative thinking on a broad range of issues relating to democratic practice and theory. An electoral democracy, to be effective, must show a strong relationship between representation and a fair open election process. Designed to foster debate and challenge assumptions about how elections and democratic representation *should* work, titles in the series will present a strong but fair argument on topics related to elections, voting behavior, party and media involvement, representation, and democratic theory.

**Rethinking American Electoral Democracy**
*Matthew J. Streb*

**Redistricting and Representation: Why Competitive Elections are Bad for America**
*Thomas L. Brunell*

# Redistricting and Representation

## Why Competitive Elections are Bad for America

Thomas L. Brunell

Routledge
Taylor & Francis Group

NEW YORK AND LONDON

First published 2008
by Routledge
270 Madison Ave, New York, NY 10016

Simultaneously published in the UK
by Routledge
2 Park Square, Milton Park, Abingdon, Oxon OX14 4RN

*Routledge is an imprint of the Taylor & Francis Group,
an informa business*

© 2008 Taylor & Francis Group

Typeset in Galliard by RefineCatch Limited, Bungay, Suffolk
Printed and bound in the United States of America on acid-free
paper by Walsworth Publishing Company, Marceline, MO

*Library of Congress Cataloging in Publication Data*
Brunell, Thomas L. (Thomas Lloyd)
Redistricting and representation : why competitive elections are
bad for America / by Thomas L. Brunell. – 1st ed.
    p. cm. – (Controversies in electoral democracy and
representation)
ISBN 978-0-415-96452-4 (hardback : alk. paper) –
ISBN 978-0-415-96453-1 (pbk. : alk. paper) –
ISBN 978-0-203-92972-8 (ebook) 1. Elections–United States.
2. Political campaigns–United States. I. Title.
JK1976.B74 2008
324.973–dc22

                                                    2007040874


ISBN10: 0–415–96452–0 (hbk)
ISBN10: 0–415–96453–9 (pbk)
ISBN10: 0–203–92972–1 (ebk)


ISBN13: 978–0–415–96452–4 (hbk)
ISBN13: 978–0–415–96453–1 (pbk)
ISBN10: 978–0–203–92972–8 (ebk)

To my parents, Ron and Carol
To my children, Max and Nate
And to my lovely wife, Valerie

# Contents

# Preface

This idea for this book was planted in the back of my mind several years ago when I was an assistant professor at Binghamton University. Chris Anderson was working on his winners/losers research and it occurred to me at the time that competitive elections necessarily mean there are many losing voters, which, as Chris was showing with his work, is a negative development. At the time there was, to the best of my knowledge, nobody arguing that competitive elections have serious downsides in any way, shape, or form. The idea germinated in my mind for several years while I occasionally thought about the real implications of competitive elections for representation and voting. It took that long to convince myself that I wasn't crazy to think that uncompetitive elections might actually be better than competitive ones. Eventually I decided to begin analyzing some data and putting my thoughts down on paper. You now hold the final product of this work.

Somewhere in the middle of all of this I learned that there was, in fact, another political scientist making an argument similar to mine. My first instinct was that I might get scooped by this person—ironic to have such a competitive reaction when I was arguing against competition. I found out that it was a newly minted Ph.D. from Berkeley named Justin Buchler and I wrote to him about his work and my ideas. This began a long on-going conversation about competition and representation. While we agreed with one another on the subject, we were taking slightly different approaches to the question. Rather than competing with one another trying to scoop the other, we ended up collaborating on a paper and gave each other advice on our various papers. Given the fact that most people, political scientists or otherwise, do not have particularly warm reactions to the idea that we need less electoral competition, it was nice to find a sympathetic ear.

Some of these negative reactions are worth noting. I presented my argument at the annual meeting of the American Political Science Association one year and a member of the audience was so incensed at my suggestion that we further reduce competition in congressional elections that he accused me of spreading dangerous ideas! At another conference a famous political scientist called some of my ideas "cockamamie." Another highly regarded political scientist remarked, after seeing me present my argument at two conferences, that he was very suspect of "Tom Brunell's traveling comedy show." He called it a comedy show because I have a sense of humor and I had some good jokes that day, but also because, like in any good comedy, I think he saw some nuggets of truth in my arguments. The paper that ended up being published in *PS* was originally submitted to another journal where it was rejected, in part, because one anonymous reviewer was convinced that the entire 30 page article with tons of supporting data was written "tongue in cheek, à la Jonathan Swift's *A Modest Proposal*." The idea that more competition is always better is deeply ingrained in our culture. Given this history, I do want to assure the reader that none of what I have written in this book is intended to be tongue-in-cheek. I understand why most people will initially have a visceral reaction against my argument and I also take some comfort in an old maxim by philosopher Arthur Schopenhauer: "All truth passes through three stages. First, it is ridiculed. Second, it is violently opposed. Third, it is accepted as being self-evident." This idea is still somewhere between stages one and two.

Like every author, I have a long list of people that I need to acknowledge for their help somewhere along the way of writing this book. Jim Adams, Chris Anderson, Clark Bensen, Patrick Brandt, Valerie Brunell, Justin Buchler, Bruce Cain, Harold Clarke, Liz Clausen, Russ Dalton, David Flaherty, Morris Fiorina, Ted Harpham, Tom Hofeller, Bill Koetzle, David Lublin, Michael D. McDonald, Michael P. McDonald, Sam Merrill, Joel Olson, Glenn Phelps, David Rueda, Scott Steiner, Marianne Stewart, Matt Streb, and Carole Wilson all helped me at some point during this project. I owe a special debt of gratitude to Bernie Grofman—he continues to be a great advisor, co-author, and friend. I also have to acknowledge that Clark Bensen of Polidata.org has been exceedingly generous with his time, maps, and data. Not only for this book but over the years for many different projects Clark has been a great help and he created the maps of Georgia's congressional districts in chapter 4. My wife, Valerie, created the figures in chapter 4 for contiguity and compactness. Suffice it to say, she has a future in drawing districts. In addition, Richard Niemi, University of Rochester; Bruce Cain, University of California Berkeley; David Lublin, American University; and John L. Korey, California State Polytechnic University Pomona all offered constructive and helpful comments in their reviews of my proposal and early draft chapters.

It is safe to say that with one exception (Justin Buchler) there is nobody on the list above that necessarily agrees with my argument. In fact, much more likely, all of them disagree with what I say in this book, at least, in part. Nonetheless there is nothing more satisfying than hashing out ideas with smart and interesting people, and I am grateful to each of them for their time and thoughts.

# Chapter 1

# Introduction

On November 2, 2004 President George W. Bush was reelected to serve another four years in the White House. While the election was relatively close by historical standards, it was not the cliff-hanger that the country witnessed four years prior. Part of the election post-mortem was a discussion of the Blue State blues in which Democratic voters who were really hoping to end Bush's reign on Pennsylvania Avenue were depressed due to the outcome of the election. Senator John Kerry lost and the Democrats would be stuck with a Republican president for four more years.

Three days after the election, National Public Radio devoted a segment on their *Talk of the Nation* program to the discussion of post-election stress.[1] Doctor Emmanuel Maidenberg, a clinical psychologist from UCLA, was interviewed on the program and while he had not seen any academic studies done on the topic, he was convinced from his clinical experience that there was a real depression among people who had been hopeful that Kerry would win the election. One of the callers to the show said that the result was especially depressing because so many people did not think Bush had really won the election in 2000 and they had already waited four years to get rid of him and were now facing another four years before the next opportunity to elect a candidate that they prefer.

During this time, there were tales of liberals joining together to drown their sorrows at the local pub; or even people so fed up with President Bush that they were going to move to Canada. Indeed, in the days following the election it was reported that traffic on the Canadian immigration website more than tripled and that hundreds of Americans were paying $25 to attend seminars on Canadian immigration.[2] There were also reports that some Hollywood celebrities, such as Alec Baldwin, were promising to move to Europe if President Bush were reelected. While this mass exodus may not have actually happened, it is important to note the degree to which voters on the losing side were extremely disappointed and upset.

Electoral competition, like all other forms of competition, has winners and losers. And, naturally, losers are less happy with the result than the winners. This is true both for candidates who are running for office and for the voters who cast their ballots on Election Day. There is not much that can be done to reduce the proportion of losing voters in American presidential elections since there can only be one president and the electoral boundaries of the country remain static from election to election. For the last decade or so the country has been divided fairly evenly between Democrats and Republicans (or as it has become more popular to talk in terms of colors, between blue voters and red voters, respectively). While there is an active debate over whether or not the American public is polarized,[3] virtually everyone agrees that the nation is roughly evenly divided between the two major parties.[4] Given this divide, it is impossible for everyone to be pleased with the outcome of a presidential election, but the same is not true for all other elected officials to the state governments or the federal government. There is something we can do to improve the relative proportion of winners and losers in terms of elections to the House of Representatives and state legislative elections around the country. Rather than drawing districts to try to maximize the likelihood that elections will be competitive between the two major parties in the general election, we could draw districts with as little ideological diversity as possible to maximize the number of winning voters, and thereby, minimize the number of losing voters.

The issues taken up in this book include:

- Are voters in Congressional elections more satisfied with the outcome when the candidate that they vote for actually wins the election?
- Are winning voters more likely to be satisfied with their representation in Congress than losing voters?
- Are they more satisfied with Congress as an institution?

The answer to all of these questions is an unqualified "yes." While this finding is interesting, it is not earth-shattering news to be told that "voters whose preferred candidate won the election are happier than the losing voters." However, what is quite provocative are the implications from these findings with respect to the process of redistricting in the United States; namely, districts should not be drawn to maximize competitiveness, the approach commonly assumed to be best, but instead should be drawn in such a way that they are "packed" with as many like-minded partisans in each district as possible.

## The redistricting process

Every ten years a census of the American population is taken—a process mandated in Article 1, Section 2 of the U.S. Constitution. Originally, the results of the census were used to reapportion the House of Representatives, whereby states gain seats and others lose seats in the House based on their relative share of the population.[5] While the House is still reapportioned today, the much more interesting and politically charged process that happens after each census involves the redrawing of congressional and state legislative district lines which occurs after the seats in House have been redistributed based on population changes.

The redistricting process happens at the state level, although there are many federal implications as well, including the Voting Rights Act and numerous Supreme Court decisions that affect what can be done in the map-making process. Each state with more than one seat in the House of Representatives must create a new map for their congressional delegation after every census, and all 50 states must draw new district lines for their state legislative bodies. While there are different processes by which states undertake the process of redistricting, the most common approach essentially boils down to passing a piece of legislation that delineates what the districts will look like for the next decade. Since the process involves political outcomes and since elected officials are at the heart of the process, naturally there is a significant amount of partisanship in the process. Some states, such as New Jersey and Iowa, try to make the process somewhat less partisan by involving bipartisan commissions to draw the new boundaries. While it is not possible to take the politics out of redistricting, it is possible to take the politicians out of redistricting. While some people think that this approach will lead to better electoral districts, it is not clear that any procedural reforms necessarily lead to better districts.[6] District lines are artificial—it is impossible to tell, when driving across the interstate, when one has left one congressional or state legislative district and crossed into another. This artificiality gives us great flexibility in how we draw district lines. While there are some principles that guide how we draw district lines (which are covered in-depth in chapter 4), there is a significant amount of latitude in what congressional and state legislative districts end up looking like. Indeed, some folks think there is too much flexibility, which allows the elected officials who draw these lines to use this flexibility for devious and partisan purposes.

The term "gerrymandering" comes to us thanks to the actions of the Governor of Massachusetts, Elbridge Gerry, circa 1810–11. While Mr. Gerry had an incredibly distinguished career in early American politics—he was a signatory on the Declaration of Independence, he was a member of the Continental Congress, he attended the Constitutional Convention in Philadelphia, he was elected to the House of Representatives, and he died as the vice president of the United States serving under James Madison—he will be remembered as the man who engineered an oddly shaped district in his state to favor an incumbent from his own party. A famous political cartoon was drawn that showed the district to be in the shape of a salamander. Since then, pundits and politicians alike have invented ever more fanciful names or descriptions for districts with less-than-straight lines. In the 2002 map drawn by Pennsylvania Republicans, opponents referred to two different districts as a "supine seahorse" and an "upside down Chinese dragon."[7] California Governor Arnold Schwarzenegger, who headed a well-publicized but ultimately failed campaign to reform the redistricting process in the Golden State, remarked about his own state's districts that some look like they were drawn by "a drunk with an Etch-A-Sketch."[8] Appearances do matter in redistricting and districts with rather tortured shapes invite derision from opposing political parties and the media.

While we may simply associate gerrymandering with districts that are oddly shaped, the meaning of the term has changed to mean something more nuanced. Modern gerrymandering involves one political party drawing districts in such a way that they dilute the votes of the other party and are thus enabling themselves to win more seats in Congress or in the state legislature than they would under different districting plan. Oddly shaped districts can be an indication that one party has gerrymandered the other, but funny-looking districts are neither necessary nor sufficient to enact a gerrymander. Depending on how voters are distributed across a state, one party can really put the other party at a significant disadvantage with nicely shaped districts which are pleasing to the eye. And on the other side of the coin, while really weird districts may mean something is amiss, a perfectly reasonable district plan can be drawn with jagged district lines that appear to have been drawn by a preschooler. The shape or appearance of electoral districts is significantly less important than the demographic and partisan composition of the districts.

Partisan gerrymandering is surely one of the biggest threats to a properly functioning American Congress. District plans ought to reflect the underlying partisanship of the state and any distortions from this reflection are unfair and undemocratic. This is particularly critical when you consider the fact that the founders of this country designed the House of Representatives to be the institution in the federal government that should most closely reflect the will of the people. Originally the House was the only part of the federal government that was directly elected by the people themselves. The president has always been elected indirectly through the Electoral College (and it is important to note that in many states the legislature picked their electors, which meant that "the people" had no direct say whatsoever in terms of who would be president). Senators were elected from each state by their respective state legislatures until the ratification of the Seventeenth Amendment to the Constitution in 1913 which provided for their popular election. And the entire federal judiciary is appointed to lifetime terms. Moreover, the House represents the people, and thus seats were divided among the states according to their share of the population. Finally, in order to ensure that those people who were elected to the House remained faithful to the constituencies that elected them, the founders provided for the shortest terms between elections in the House—just two years. John Adams said of the House of Representatives, "It should be in miniature, an exact portrait of the people at large." While we can immediately discard the notion that any elected body could be "an exact portrait" of the people, the point is still quite important—the House of Representatives, more than any other federal governmental institution, should most closely represent the people of the country. Gerrymandering distorts the translation of votes into seats, and therefore threatens to turn the House of Representatives into what Sam Hirsch calls "the House of Unrepresentatives."[9] A fundamental question to address then is how should the House of Representatives best mirror the population? Over the years there have been many different theories and approaches to answering this fundamental question of what representation is and even what representation ought to be. One of the most fundamental dichotomies in the discussion of representation is trustee versus delegate. The trustee/delegate debate centers around the motivating factors that guide how the representative votes. If the representative votes based on the wishes of her constituents, since they are the reason that she is a member of Congress in the first place, then this is the delegate form of representation. On the other hand, if after someone is elected they do not tend to weigh the wishes of their constituents in their voting behavior, but rather rely on their own good judgment to vote, or they vote on the basis of what is good for the country and not necessarily what is good just for the district, then this is a representative who is acting like a trustee. In the next chapter the various notions of what representation is and what it ought to be are addressed in depth.

## Competition and redistricting

Competition is one of the underlying principles associated with the American way of life. People compete in virtually all aspects of life—from sports to business to school. Schoolchildren compete to see who can spell more words correctly than anyone else, or who is better at geography. Competition, we are taught, is universally good. Given the universality of the American appreciation for competition, it is no surprise that we highly value its presence in elections. Competitive elections are good we are told: they are good for the voters, they are good for representation, and they are good for the media that cover the elections (stories about uncontested elections are not going to sell any magazines). Moreover, without electoral competition, we are told, there is no basis for governmental responsiveness. If we do not hold elected officials feet to the fire every two years, they begin to feel very comfortable in their position and no longer care what the voters in their district think. The following quote is from the introduction of a book put together by two of the leading redistricting scholars that exemplifies the belief held by most pundits and scholars: "The essence of any democratic regime is the competitive election of officeholders. It is only by making candidates compete for their seats that politicians can be held accountable by the public."[10] The common wisdom suggests that the absence of electoral competition is an indication of a democracy at risk.

It is not particularly difficult to find hundreds of examples of people extolling the virtues of competition—consider, for example, the following from a November 10, 2002 *Washington Post* editorial:

The magnitude of incumbency's triumph in last week's elections for the

House of Representatives was so dramatic that the term "election"—with its implications of voter choice and real competition—seems almost too generous to describe what happened on Tuesday. Voters went to the polls, and they cast ballots, and they did so without coercion. Yet somehow, at the end of the day, 98 percent of House incumbents seeking reelection won—and by margins that suggest that many of the races were never serious.

Or as *The Times Union* newspaper of Albany, New York editorialized: "we need to focus more on redistricting reform. New Yorkers cannot influence the direction of government without competitive elections, and minimizing the influence of political decision making in the redistricting process will help bring this about."[11] It is clear that the common wisdom with respect to electoral competitiveness is that its absence is an indication that something is amiss with our democracy. The general sense is that politicians are drawing their own district lines which assure that they continue to be reelected by wide margins, which means that they do not have to be responsive to the wants and needs of the electorate. Virtually every incumbent wins, usually in a lopsided fashion, and the redistricting process is often portrayed as the culprit for the lack of competition. While it is clear that redistricting contributes to this process, it is not the only factor that affects competitiveness. In fact, the biggest factor affecting the competitiveness of an election, assuming an incumbent is running for reelection, is whether or not a high-quality challenger emerges to challenge the incumbent. Absent a good challenger, irrespective of what the district looks like, there will not be a competitive election.[12] And even if redistricting is to blame for the decline in competition in congressional general elections, is this decline really a problem? Competitive elections are an indication that the incumbent could be replaced, which supposedly is the main force that drives the member to actively pursue the interests of his constituents. But regardless of whether or not every election is competitive, the threat that the next election *could be* competitive is sufficient to keep members on the straight and narrow. As long as the potential exists for an incumbent member to be replaced, then responsiveness ought not to be a problem. And while it has been said before, it bears mentioning again, that noncompetitive elections could be an indication of a high degree of satisfaction with the incumbent among the voters in a district.

The desire for increased competition in American elections goes beyond the wishes of pundits and academics; various states have passed laws or amended their state constitutions to encourage the drawing of competitive districts. In 2000 the voters of the state of Arizona passed Proposition 206, which requires: "To the extent practicable, competitive districts should be favored where to do so would create no significant detriment to the other goals" (sec. 14, subsection F). Redistricting reform is a hot topic across the country and the general sense one gets is that the process of redistricting should be taken out of the hands of the state legislature and given to some other entity. Furthermore, there should be a purposeful effort to increase the amount of competition in elections when the district boundaries are changed.

In November of 2005 the voters in Ohio voted down (71 percent against, 29 percent in favor) a ballot initiative (HJR 6) that would have taken the process of redistricting out of the hands of the current partisan commission and created an "independent apportionment board" to handle the decadal task of redrawing state legislative and congressional district boundaries. There was an entire section (number 5) of the proposed reform dedicated to "adopting a redistricting plan to ensure competitive elections." The bill defined how to score different plans on their levels of competitiveness and included requirements to adopt the version with more competitive districts. In fact there was a further requirement that if no plan submitted to the commission "qualified" based on the basic redistricting and competitiveness requirements, "then the commission is required to design and adopt a plan that conforms to the required criteria and seeks to maximize the competitiveness number." So competitiveness was a centerpiece for this proposal, although a majority of the voters in Ohio decided not to pass it.

In 2005, voters in California were asked to vote on a proposition similar to the one in Ohio. Proposition 77 was one of four propositions put before the voters by Republican Governor Arnold Schwarzenegger. His strategy of putting policy reforms directly before the voters was an effort to sidestep the state legislature, which is controlled by a Democratic majority. In his state of the state speech in 2005, the governor claimed: "the current system is rigged to benefit the interests of those in office, not the interests of those who put them there. And we must reform it." His solution was to take redistricting out of the hands of the state government and give the power to a newly created independent panel of three retired judges. The specific mechanics of how the process would work are as follows. The state Judicial Council would select, by lot, a pool of 24 retired judges who had volunteered to be chosen. These judges could never have run for elected office. Representatives from both parties would winnow this field to 16. From those finalists, three would be chosen at random to comprise the three-judge panel. The voters rejected this proposal, along with the three other reform-minded propositions from the governor. So this redistricting proposal, like many others, failed at the ballot box. In this case, the unpopularity of Governor Schwarzenegger at the time undoubtedly contributed to the demise of Proposition 77.

There are even reform-minded interest groups that have weighed in on the issue of redistricting and competition. For instance, Fairvote.org is one of the more visible groups in this arena. They analyze data, write articles for the opinion pages of major newspapers, and issue reports on the current state of American democracy. One of the factors that Fairvote uses as an indication that our democracy may not be as healthy as it could be is what they call "voter choice." Clearly, a democracy without any real choice among candidates for the voters is a rather empty system. There are a fair number of uncontested general elections in the House every cycle and Fairvote takes the lack of competition at the aggregate level to mean that American voters do not have the kinds of choices that they ought to have. For instance they say "The past two House elections were the least competitive in American history by most standards. In each of the four national elections since 1996, more than 98 percent of incumbents have won, and more than 90 percent of all races have been won by noncompetitive margins of more than 10 percent."[13] While these statistics reflect the reality of modern American congressional elections, there is no reason to draw the conclusion that democracy is in trouble and that people have no control over the government based on these data. First, political scientists have demonstrated that one of the reasons that election outcomes are very uncompetitive is that incumbents who feel like they might lose the next election actually retire before this can happen.[14] This opens the door for the challenger to win by a larger margin than they would have had the incumbent stuck around and ran in the election. Cox and Katz call this phenomenon "strategic exit." The other side of this same coin is "strategic entry" where good high-quality challengers voluntarily sit on the sidelines as long as the incumbent remains in solid electoral shape. Only when the time is just right do quality candidates run against an incumbent. If these potential challengers were not strategic and ran in every election against incumbents, election outcomes would be much closer, and the aggregate measure of competitiveness would be much higher. Does this mean that voters have more choices? At some level it does, but it will not change many outcomes (i.e., incumbents will not lose many elections).

The general consensus with respect to redistricting is that there is not enough competition in congressional elections and redistricting is the likely culprit for this absence. While the voters of some states have recently turned down proposals to reform the redistricting process, it is pretty clear that the average voter is not a strong supporter of the ways in which districts are currently drawn. The public proclamations of politicians have not helped in this matter either, with a state senator from California admitting "We are politicians, and we do have the interests of incumbents at heart. There is no question about that."[15] Are independent or nonpartisan redistricting commissions a panacea for these problems? This is highly unlikely. Would these types of bodies cut down on the number of "bipartisan gerrymanders" in which the incumbents from both parties collude to protect all incumbents? They might, but the more important question is will the elimination of districts that overtly protect incumbents change anything? There might be an increase in the number of competitive elections across the country, and there may even be more turnover in the membership of the House of Representatives, but will this somehow make representatives more responsive to voters, or will voters be significantly happier with their representation in Congress? The answer to both of these questions is a definitive "no."

## A simple example

Figure 1.1 depicts two sets of hypothetical districts for a state with four congressional districts. The state is equally divided between Democrats (white) and Republicans (black). Since the state gets four seats in the House of Representatives and is equally divided between the two parties, the obvious and only "correct" outcome is one in which each party receives two seats (2D and 2R). Any deviations from this outcome are unfair and unrepresentative. These two hypothetical districting schemes can be used to conduct an "ideal type" analysis. This method, based on work by Max Weber, allows us to conduct comparative analysis of whatever it is that we are interested in by imaging our variables in their "ideal" state. It is impossible to draw districts in such a way that an entire state (or even a single district in a state) is either perfectly competitive or perfectly homogeneous. However, it is important to think about the outcomes that these two kinds of districting plans lead to and draw conclusions as to which one of these extremes is more appropriate and desirable.

The first line in Figure 1.1 indicates that all four districts have been drawn to maximize competition—each district is split right down the middle with 50 percent of the state Democratic and 50 percent Republican. The second row of districts represents a map that is perfectly homogeneous with two districts populated entirely by Republicans and two districts by Democrats. Clearly neither of these districting methods is realistically possible, but we can still imagine what kinds of outcomes are likely under these two scenarios and form judgments about which extreme case ought to be emulated when states are obliged to draw new electoral boundaries.

The competitive plan is essentially four consecutive flips of a coin with either party having a 50 percent chance of capturing any seat. This is a simple binomial distribution problem and it is easy to estimate the likely outcomes in terms of the partisanship of the seats. Listed below are each of the possible outcomes with the percentage of time that each is expected.

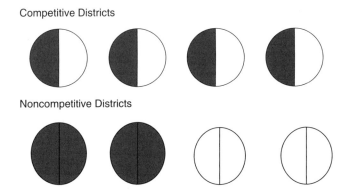

Competitive Districts

Noncompetitive Districts

*Figure 1.1* Two hypothetical redistricting plans.

- RRRR—6.25%
- RRRD—25%
- RRDD—37.5%
- DDDR—25%
- DDDD—6.25%

So 6.25 percent of the time all four seats would be carried by Republican candidates (RRRR). Half the time this representation scheme yields delegations with a three to one split (either DDDR or RRRD), which does not reflect the underlying partisanship of the state. Far worse is the fact that we expect outcomes composed entirely of one party or the other (DDDD or RRRR) fully 12.5 percent of the time, leaving half the state with no effective representation whatsoever. Recall that this state has four seats and half the state is Republican and the other half is Democratic, so the only appropriate representation for the state is one with two Republican seats and two Democratic seats. In this case, a map composed of purely competitive districts yields the "correct" answer (two seats for each party) only 37.5 percent of the time! If we want the House to be "an exact portrait" of the country like the founders envisioned, then drawing competitive districts is surely not the best way to get there. More than six times out of ten, a state composed entirely of competitive seats yields completely nonproportional representation for the state. Even when a competitive districting scheme does get the "correct" outcome, it still unnecessarily forces half the state to be represented by someone that they did not support, and presumably will not be satisfied with the voting behavior of the representative in Congress.

It is often said that competitive districts will force representatives to be more responsive to their constituents. This, however, cannot be the case. A representative of a competitive district can really only represent or be responsive to a portion of the district. By definition, a competitive district is going to include a substantial portion of the voting population that does not support the incumbent or the incumbent's political platform and will not likely approve of the votes that the representative casts in the House. As the diversity of ideologies in a district increases, this increases the likelihood of a competitive election, but, and more importantly, the possibility of an elected official being responsive declines. The common wisdom that one hears from political scientists linking more electoral competition to higher levels of responsiveness is actually backwards. It is impossible to be responsive to a district in which half of the people want higher taxes and the other half want lower taxes.

The safe district method, on the other hand, always produces representation that reflects the partisan leanings of the state. It is easy to imagine that, without fail, the homogeneous district approach elects two Democrats and two Republicans. Moreover, all the voters are happy with the partisanship of their representative. There are more conservative Republicans and more liberal Republicans, so some voters will be more satisfied than others depending on the ideology of the person elected, but still this person is from the "right" party with respect to all the voters in the district. However, it is possible for the representative to be responsive to the entire district since the constituents all belong to the same party. Voters are more satisfied with the election outcome because they are better represented in Congress. Even better, the representative's job is made easier because he receives clear, noncontradictory signals from his district as to how to vote on the issues of the day.

Competition is valued and it does serve a purpose. No one wants to see the Super Bowl end in a 42–3 blowout and no one wants to see one candidate glide to victory with 85 percent of the vote. Unless of course it is your favorite football team or your preferred candidate! For instance, USC trounced Oklahoma in the Orange Bowl 55–19 to win the national championship for the 2004 season. It was not a particularly exciting game. The next year, the Trojans lost to Texas 41–38 in what was definitely one of the most exciting football games to watch of all time. From the perspective of a USC fan though, which game was better? The game against Oklahoma to be sure. Americans like competition, but they also like to win. It turns out that the primal relationship for voting and positive attitudes toward government is whether voters cast their ballot for the winning candidate in the last election. The degree of competitiveness of that election is unimportant.

## Elections and responsiveness

The cry for more competition in House elections is so prevalent that we rarely reflect upon the costs associated with competitive elections nor do we question the link between competition and responsiveness. Political scientists have become so used to saying that "competition leads to more responsiveness" that they do not even stop to think what this means.

Critical to democratic representation is the notion that the government remains responsive to the wishes of the electorate.[16] Elections are the fundamental, although not the only, method of keeping our elected officials faithful to the public. In order to take office and remain in office, members of the House of Representatives have to stand before their constituents every two years and seek their approval. This electoral process is the keystone of representative government. Why do elections encourage, or even force representatives to carry out the wishes of the electorate? Elections work because they plant a degree of uncertainty in the mind of the representative as to whether she will be able to keep her job. Being a member of Congress is a highly valued position, and very rarely do we witness members leaving office voluntarily, despite the fact that they would win the next election.[17] So someone occupying a seat in the House values keeping their position since it pays fairly well, they have a certain amount of power, and they can affect the federal laws and most important public policies of the country to list just a few reasons. The catch, however, is that in order to keep this fantastic job, the incumbent has to get more votes than any other person running for the office in the district every two years. Even though most incumbents who do run, end up winning the election, that does not mean that there is not some uncertainty in their minds as to whether or not they will win the election. The threat of defeat is still there, and this threat or uncertainty is what keeps members faithful, not the presence of a competitive general election.

One aspect of the American electoral system that differs from most of the world is that voters actually get two opportunities to pass judgment on their representatives biannually. First, politicians have to win a primary election, securing their party's nomination for the general election, and, second, they must also win the general election against an opponent from the other party. This works in the voters' favor because it means that no incumbent is truly safe. If someone represents an overwhelming Democratic district, and is virtually guaranteed victory in the general election, there is still a chance that they may face electoral defeat during the primary election at the hands of a fellow Democrat. Therefore despite the fact that the district will never see a competitive general election, the incumbent is not without some degree of uncertainty about keeping the seat because a good primary challenger can still emerge if the incumbent fails to do his job (i.e., represent the wishes of his constituency). In the 2006 election cycle there were a number of high profile incumbents defeated in the primary election stage: Joe Lieberman (D-CT) lost the Democratic primary, but given the lack of "sore loser" laws in Connecticut, which prevent candidates who lose the primary from running in the general election as an Independent, he was able to keep his seat in the Senate anyhow. Frank Murkowski, the incumbent Republican governor of Alaska, finished last in a three person Republican primary. Cynthia McKinney (D-GA) lost her seat in the House at the primary stage. So incumbents do lose primary elections, not at particularly high rates, but we only need a few examples of incumbents tossed out by the primary electorate to keep the rest of the members heeding our wishes. Drawing districts to maximize the odds of having a competitive general election then is not a requirement for a healthy, well-functioning, democratic Congress. The more important the primary, that is, the more lopsided the district is in favor of one party or the other, the more likely the primary election will be contested and turnout will be higher.[18]

## Losers and winners

Another important aspect to competition is that the process yields both winners and losers. Only one team wins the World Series. Only one child wins the spelling bee. Only one candidate wins each elective office. But the outcome affects more than just the participants—it affects people that care about the competition and those that are competing. When the Dallas Cowboys win the Super Bowl there are millions of happy Cowboys fans, but there are also millions of fans who were rooting for the losing team that are fairly disappointed. Similarly, when a Democrat wins election to the House of Representatives, there are tens of thousands of satisfied voters who cast their ballot for this candidate, but there are also many supporters of the Republican (albeit fewer than for the Democrat) who are upset with the outcome.

Having competitive general elections in House races involves drawing the boundaries in such a way that the proportion of voters who lean toward the Democratic Party is roughly equal to the proportion of voters who prefer a Republican. The district needs to be comprised in such a way that prospective high-quality candidates from both parties think that they have a reasonable chance to win the general election. If the district leans toward one party or the other, a quality candidate from the disadvantaged party is likely to decide not to run at all. Let's assume that two high-quality candidates do emerge and both run great campaigns. Only one candidate can win and this leaves a sub-stantial portion of the population dissatisfied with the outcome. This means that we need to seriously consider the costs associated with drawing districts that maximize the likelihood that we will have a competitive general election. Put simply, drawing competitive districts optimizes the number of losers (i.e., the number of dissatisfied voters). The opening of this chapter detailed the unhappiness that millions of Americans felt after the presidential election in 2004. Should we try to recreate this extreme unhappiness in each of the 435 House districts (and thousands of state legislative districts) across the country? Losing voters, the data will demonstrate, are less satisfied with the representa-tive from their district, less satisfied with Congress as a whole, have lower feelings of efficaciousness, and have less trust in government. Moreover it is this winner–loser distinction, and not how competitive the election, that profoundly affects voters' attitudes toward government.

The fact that we can keep representatives responsive to our wishes even if the district is safe, combined with the fact that competitive elections optimize the number of unhappy voters, suggests a profound need for a fundamental rethinking of how to approach redistricting. In this book I argue that we ought to be decreasing the amount of general election competitiveness to maximize the number of satisfied voters. Rather than drawing 50–50 districts, we should be drawing districts that are overwhelmingly comprised of one party or the other (80–20 or even 90–10) to whatever extent possible. This substantially increases the number of voters who will be both happier with their representa-tive and better served by this representative. This comes at no reduction in the level of faithfulness by the representatives as they remain uncertain about being reelected due to competition at the primary election stage. But is increasing happiness or utility sufficient to warrant this radical departure from traditional districting methods? Congress is traditionally low-man on the totem pole when it comes to favorable ratings from the American public. Both the Supreme Court and the Presidency are systematically rated more favorably by voters.[19] Increasing satisfaction among the people with Congress certainly cannot hurt and, more likely, any increase will have a positive effect.

But this approach to redistricting also has other significant benefits associated with it beyond simply pleasing more voters. Packing districts with as many Democrats or as many Republicans as possible makes it virtually certain that the distribution of seats between the two parties from each state will approximate the underlying partisan division of voters. This is to say a state with twice as many Democrats than Republicans will end up with twice as many seats held by Democrats than Republicans. Gerrymandering, as I stated above, is the purposeful mistranslation of votes into seats that advantages one party (and disadvantages the other party) and using this new approach to draw district lines will make it much more difficult to gerrymander a state.[20]

Creating homogeneous congressional and state legislative districts will also strengthen the connections between the people and the elected officials. Much of the social science literature on the subject of constituency control over elected officials suggests a rather weak relationship. For instance, most voters have virtually no idea about how their representative is voting in Congress. Furthermore, incumbents have a rather feeble idea about the real preferences of their constituents. As Miller and Stokes put it in their classic article: "The Representative has very imperfect information about the issue preferences of his constituency, and the constituency's awareness of the policy stands of the Representative ordinarily is slight."[21] By making districts more homogeneous we necessarily make the translation of voter preferences into public policy more likely because the representative will have a more clear idea of how the district leans on any single issue. Moreover, given the ideological homogeneity of the district, it gives the elected official less wiggle room in their voting calculus. If all the voters in the district want a "yes" vote on a certain bill, there is no place to hide if the incumbent decides to vote "nay."

Here I make the case against competitive elections in Congress (and by analogy to state legislative districts as well) arguing that competitive districts maximize the proportion of losers in the country. Convincing others that this is right will be a tough row to hoe given the prevalence of the view that what the country lacks, more than anything else in modern elections, is competition. At the very least I hope to convey the notion that there are very significant costs to trying to create competition using the process of redistricting. In my mind these costs far outweigh the benefits, which is why I am putting forward an innovative approach to how we ought to draw election district boundaries.

## Layout of the book

Chapter 2 reviews some of the prior work done on political representation and explicates the straightforward form of representation that I use in the remainder of the book. Chapter 3 contains the analyses of decades of survey data where I show that people like to win elections and competition does not matter all that much. For those readers who prefer not to get bogged down by digesting tables of statistical analyses, this chapter can be skipped. Chapter 4 is a review of the guiding principles involved in the redistricting process. Here each principle is laid out for the reader and I address how a fair partisan plan (the approach advocated in this book) would work with each of these principles. Chapter 5 lays out the benefits to this new approach to redistricting and Chapter 6 addresses many of the criticisms that have been leveled at my approach. Chapter 7 concludes.

# Chapter 2

# Theories of representation

On its face the concept of representation seems simple—one person acts on behalf of others. But as one scratches the surface of representation, the concept becomes significantly more complex. How should one person represent others? Should she do what she thinks is right? Should she do what most of her constituents think is right? Perhaps she should do what is best for the larger community (state, nation, world) rather than what is best for just the people she represents. Should a representative look like the constituency or act like the constituency? It is fundamentally a complex notion, moreover on top of this complexity is another layer of normative conceptions regarding how representation ought to work.

As everyone who has taken an Introduction to American Government class knows, historically scholars (and politicians) have disagreed as to whether a political representative ought to act as a trustee or a delegate. Simply put, if a representative is acting as a delegate he is merely acting and voting in the way in which his constituency prefers. On the other hand, a trustee is someone who, rather than consulting or even listening to his constituency, acts in a fashion that he feels is best (based on his own judgment). Underlying this dichotomy is the question: how much independence does a representative get or deserve (from his constituents)? Should a representative act simply as a fiduciary, responsible for translating the preferences of constituents into action as accurately and faithfully as possible? Or do citizens elect people of "distinction" in whom they have faith to "do the right thing?"[1] In reality it is likely that virtually every elected representative sometimes acts as a trustee and other times as a delegate. If a member of Congress is voting on something that his constituents have no preference about or are indifferent between the two choices, the elected official makes a decision based on other factors (e.g. his own ideology, interest group lobbying, deal-making, etc.).

Regardless of how one approaches the concept of representation, it is clear that electing representatives is one of the most significant forms of democratic action that citizens can have. Robert Dahl puts it nicely in trying to describe how best to design a democracy: "The only feasible solution, though it is highly imperfect, is for citizens to elect their top officials and hold them more or less accountable through elections by dismissing them, so to speak, in subsequent elections."[2] Dahl goes on to list several criteria that elections must meet: "every citizen must have an equal and effective opportunity to vote, and all votes must be counted as equal. Free elections mean citizens can go to the polls unconcerned about reprisal and fair means each vote weighted equally."[3] In this chapter I review some of the current theories of political representation and then present my own approach. My approach is not necessarily new or novel, but it is straightforward and intuitive.

Pitkin's (1967) views on representation have played a major role in shaping the way in which scholars conceptualize what representation is and what it ought to be. In *The Concept of Representation*, she offers four different views and definitions of representation: formalistic representation, descriptive representation, symbolic representation, and substantive representation. Each of these provides different views of what representation is, as well as different criteria for assessing how well a representative represents her constituents. Each is worth examining in turn.

Formalistic representation, as Pitkin defines it, really has two dimensions. The first has to do with authorization and is defined "in terms of a transaction that takes place at the outset, before the actual representation begins."[4] Someone is authorized to do something via some set of institutional arrangements, but there are limits to what the representative can do. Within the competences of the initial authorization the "representative can do whatever he pleases," but if the representative does something outside of the prescribed limits, Pitkin says that "he no longer represents." The second dimension of formal representation is related to accountability. Here the central notion of representation revolves around holding the elected official accountable for what he has done. So the representative ought to be responsive to his constituents and the constituents ought to have some method of sanctioning the representative (such as removing him from office). Pitkin argues that these two forms of formal representation are in a sense diametrically opposed to one another—"whereas authorization theorists see the representative as free, the represented as bound, accountability theorists see precisely the converse."[5]

Descriptive representation, according to Pitkin, involves "standing for" the represented and does not involve acting for them. This is "by virtue of correspondence or connection between them, resemblance or reflection."[6] She goes on to say that "in political terms, what seems important is less what the legislature does than how it is composed."[7] In the American case we often refer to descriptive representation when talking about racial minorities or women being elected to Congress. When African–American voters are able to elect an African–American representative to Congress, one of the tangible benefits involves the fact that someone who looks like them (the voters) is serving in the U.S. Congress. Naturally, descriptive representation is not only defined by race or gender, there are many different aspects of one person or another that may appeal to people in terms of descriptive representation, including ideology. The legislature has a mirror-like quality with descriptive representation, it is the country in miniature, and it reflects both the good and the bad aspects of the country. But missing from this model of representation is any notion of authorization or accountability. For Pitkin, descriptive representation boils down to "representing meaning being like you, not acting for you"[8] and since the representative looks like you, he cannot be held accountable for what he does, as his similarity to the represented remains static.

Next we turn to symbolic representation in which we see "all representation as a kind of symbolization, so that a political representative is to be understood on the model of a flag representing the nation, or an emblem representing a cult."[9] Political symbols are important. The queen plays a role in the way in which English people think and feel about their country and government. While elected political leaders may be less symbolic than royalty, they still do fulfill this role.

Substantive representation involves one person acting for others, which is to say someone is acting in the interest of others, or behaving like an agent for others. Representatives vote, speak, and behave in such a way as to transmit the policy preferences of their constituents and "good" representation can be measured to the extent that the interests of the constituency have been served by the action of the elected representative.

Eulau and Karps argue that there are four components "which, as a whole, constitute representation."[10] These four are policy responsiveness, service responsiveness, allocation responsiveness, and symbolic responsiveness. We can take each in turn. Policy responsiveness is what we generally think of when we talk about representation—to what degree is the representative turning public sentiment, in her district, into public policy. This "concurrence", as Verba and Nie[11] put it, can happen purely by luck—the constituent and the representative happen to agree. It could happen because of the electoral connection, or it could be that the member of Congress was originally elected because of her policy positions. The idea of policy responsiveness can get ugly rather quickly as one begins to peel layers of the onion away. For instance, should a representative be responsive to the wishes of his constituency if the representative knows that what the district wants is wrong (in some sense of the word)? Is the public competent enough in terms of complex policy issues to really send meaningful signals about what is good for the country and what makes good public policy? For instance, immigration is a hot topic at the moment and some Americans feel very strongly about this issue. How many regular citizens really know the impact of immigrants from Central America on joblessness in the United States? Or maybe it does not matter that the public does not have a full appreciation for the complexities of immigration policy on the economy because even economists who study this issue do not agree on what policy is best.

Second is service responsiveness, which is the "nonlegislative services" that the representative provides to the constituency. The federal government is a hulking bureaucracy that individual citizens must navigate from time to time, often without much success. At times, elected officials intervene on behalf of the people that they represent to solve bureaucratic problems. An example that is often cited is when grandma fails to get her monthly Social Security check and she calls her congressman's district office to get help tracking down the money. Representatives love to do this kind of work because it is a no lose situation for them. There is nothing partisan about this "case work" and quite often the elected official's staff can rectify problems for their grateful constituents.

Allocation responsiveness refers to that part of a representative's job in which he secures federal funds for projects in the district. Today one hears about "pork-barrel projects" or "earmarks," these are the thousands of different things that the federal government funds each and every year. The sheer number and variety of these projects funded by Congress is mind-boggling. The American taxpayers have funded bicycle trails, museum renovations, the building of bridges and freeways, and academic studies to improve the shelf life of vegetables. Suffice it to say, these projects are very popular with both elected officials and constituents from both parties. One might guess that the party of small government, the Republicans, might not allocate pork like the spendthrift Democrats, but nothing could be further from the truth. Projects, such as casework, really have no enemies. The constituents view their projects as great benefits from the federal government that the representative was able to secure for them, and though some voters complain about runaway spending, when money for a new bridge comes fast and easy from Washington, most locals are not going to complain too loudly.

Lastly, is symbolic responsiveness, which is a softer and more abstract concept than the previous three. Eulau and Karps write "The representational relationship is not, however, just one of such concrete transactions, but also one that is built on trust and confidence expressed in the support that the represented give to the representative and to which he responds by symbolic, significant gestures, in order to, in turn, generate and maintain continuing support."[12] Symbolism is important for both politics and governance. Politicians use symbolism all the time to try to connect to the people. President Jimmy Carter famously wore a cardigan sweater while at work because he was setting an example for the whole country to turn down the heater in the winter to save on energy production. Adlai Stevenson, who ran unsuccessfully for president twice in the 1950s against Dwight D. Eisenhower, wore a pair of dress shoes with a hole in the sole. The fact that he had the hole and did not bother getting it fixed symbolized that Stevenson was a common man, and likeable. Politicians go to church, go hunting, eat corndogs at the county fair, and these are all aspects of symbolic representation.

Eulau and Karps argue that all four of these forms of responsiveness make up representation, and while I agree that all four play a role, I argue that two of them are more important than the others. Service and allocation responsiveness are related to the tremendous growth of the federal government over time. The federal government did not pay for walking trails in the eighteenth century and it was small enough that the average citizen did not need help navigating it if they ever had the occasion to interact with the government. It is only because the government is so large and does so much that these two functions have become part of what representatives do. Moreover, both are noncontroversial and nonpartisan, which is to say that no one is going to be upset if a staffer helps a constituent with a federal application for a grant that got lost, or if the representative brings in federal dollars to the local university. All representatives engage in this kind of behavior to some degree or another, and therefore there is not much variation across representatives. If every office engages in casework at some bare minimum level of competency, then we need not concern ourselves with it from a perspective of evaluating representation because everyone does a decent job at it. Symbolic politics, while central, is also less important than policy responsiveness in my mind. Again, since all representatives *try* to engage in this kind of responsiveness, as a concept it is less important when we try to evaluate representation across districts. There are subtleties involved in this aspect of representation that are important, such as racial descriptive representation, or electing the first female Speaker of the House. These things are important and really do affect the way people look at and evaluate government. Nonetheless, for the purposes of this book, we can relegate these three aspects of representation to the back burner and focus on the last remaining one—policy responsiveness. Policy responsiveness goes to the heart of representation. Policy and symbolic are the higher forms of representation and they are much more critical to the notion of representing someone than securing federal dollars to revamp the local bus depot.

Andrew Rehfeld has recently put forward a provocative idea of his own with respect to representation.[13] In his book *The Concept of Constituency* he presents a strong argument against using geography at all when it comes to electoral districts. For Rehfeld the ideal district in any representation scheme should have the following three characteristics: stability, involuntary membership, and heterogeneity. From these premises he shows that single-member, territorial-based districts, such as those used in the United States and many other countries, are sub-optimal. Here one would assume that Rehfeld is probably headed toward endorsing some sort of system of proportional representation (PR), where voters cast ballots for their preferred party, and the parties are allocated seats in the legislature proportional to their share of the vote nationwide. But this is not the case, because PR systems create sub-constituencies that do not meet any of the three critical criteria mentioned above. Rather, Rehfeld endorses a unique method of populating districts—citizens are randomly assigned to a congressional district at birth (or at the time they first register to vote) *for life*. These kinds of districts do meet the three characteristics that Rehfeld argues are paramount.

Each district in this kind of districting scheme would more or less be a mirror image of the country as a whole. Dividing the country's population up randomly into 435 groups and have each elect a single person. Presumably each district would elect a representative at or near the median voter in that district. Moreover, the median voter in each of these districts would not be very different from the median voter in each of the other 434 districts. Thus, every member approximates the ideology of the median voter nationwide. Theoretically, every bill should pass without dispute. While this almost certainly would not be the case, there would certainly be less deliberation and less rancor in the House.

I am not sure that when the founders argued that the House of Representatives should be a miniature replica of the country, that this is what they had in mind. By randomizing constituents into the 435 districts, Rehfeld tries to make *every district* in the House be a miniature version of the country. Traditionally we think of the House of Representatives mirroring the population not at the district level, but in the aggregate. One of the justifications for having single-member districts in the first place is to allow for local differences. Suffice it to say that there are many different ways to aggregate preferences and none is without its own problems. But Rehfeld's approach is not superior in my mind because it eliminates the diversity of race, region, ideology, etc. at the district level (i.e., the randomness of district assignments will make each district look very much like all the others). Moreover assuming that randomization works perfectly, each district should elect someone that is very nearly identical to the people elected in every other district—the median voter in each district should be very near the position of the median voter nationwide. Assume the Republicans have a slight edge in partisan identifiers in the country (53 to 47), they would control all 435 seats in the House of Representatives. Moreover it is unclear that these Republicans would be moderate at all. Both Fiorina[14] and Huntington[15] argue that in narrowly contested districts you will not see any moderation, but you will see partisan extremism. This is because the official has to pick one side or the other and treat that as their reelection constituency. Losing even a handful of votes among these people means losing one's seat.

Joseph Schumpeter[16] was an early critic of the classical theory of democracy in which voters make informed and rational decisions among candidates for office and, in turn, create public policy. His impression of average people's ability to understand and make meaningful decisions about public policy is extremely low. Indeed, he goes so far as to say that any sense of reality among these deliberations is essentially lost.[17] He even distinguishes between politics of parochial things that may matter to many people, but when it comes to more important substantive subjects, he argues that most people do not have the wherewithal or desire to fully understand what is going on. His argument is not based on limitations of cognitive ability, but rather the lack of willingness of ordinary people to engage in and think about politics. He writes: "Ignorance will persist in the face of masses of information however complete and correct. People cannot be carried up the ladder."[18]

Schumpeter's solution is a nuanced form of democracy in which there is an institutional arrangement for arriving at political decisions in which individuals acquire the power to decide by means of a competitive struggle for the people's vote.[19] Voters make quick and easy decisions about representation based on a limited choice set during an election and the primary function of the electorate is to produce a government. Citizens can then accept a leader or group of leaders or withdraw their support. The only control citizens have over such leaders is to not accept them. So leaders are truly leading—they are setting the agenda and making policy decisions that may or may not reflect what the people want. In most instances, from Schumpeter's point of view, the average voter is not going to have a preference on a complicated issue of national policy. How should a representative vote on an upcoming energy bill? Most voters (and probably lots of members of Congress) do not have even a simple appreciation for what the bill will do if it is passed. Clearly, Schumpeter has a problem with classic conceptions of democracy. For instance he writes:

> Whoever accepts the classical doctrine of democracy and in consequence believes that the democratic method is to guarantee that issues be decided and policies framed according to the will of the people must be struck by the fact that, even if that will were undeniably real and definite, decision by simple majorities would in many cases distort it rather than give effect to it. Evidently the will of the majority is the will of the majority and not the will of "the people." The latter is a mosaic that the former completely fails to "represent." To equate both by definition is not to solve the problem.[20]

Thus, Schumpeter is not particularly optimistic that translating what the "people" want can be achieved in any really sophisticated and substantive way, but rather they can choose among competing elites who are running for office and thus, affect the direction of government at a very basic level.

## A simple model of representation

Representation at its most basic level is a dyadic relationship—one between the elected representative and the individual voter. The representative will cast votes in Congress and make statements about public policy on behalf of this voter. The individual is then more or less satisfied with how well the elected official *represents* her own views in this capacity. It is unlikely that any individual voter who is fully informed about what the representative has done in Congress will be perfectly satisfied with the representative's actions. Which is to say the odds are rather low that every vote and every action taken by the representative will corresponded exactly to how the individual voter would have acted if she were elected to Congress herself. It should be clear from this discussion that policy responsiveness is central to my model of representation. This dyadic relationship is more broadly classified by economists and political scientists as a principal–agent problem. The extent to which the representative deviates from the ideal point of the voter is properly called "agency loss." Imagine the representative casts ten votes while in Congress and the voter would have cast the same votes on nine of these ten bills, agency loss for this relationship is the vote on the one bill that the voter had a different preference.

While representation at its base is a dyadic relationship, in all cases of political representation it is really an aggregation of dyadic relationships. This is to say that elected officials do not represent one person, but rather thousands or even millions of people at one time. As mentioned above, it is unlikely that a single voter will not experience some amount of agency loss (i.e., the odds of the elected official doing everything exactly the way the voter would is rather low), and it is even more evident that in the aggregate there will be a significant amount of agency loss as well.

We can judge how well an entire constituency is being represented by the elected official by the cumulative amount of agency loss that the voters experience. For instance, perfect representation with no agency loss suffered by any of the constituents would be the (clearly hypothetical) case in which the member of Congress votes *exactly* the way in which every single constituent preferred. The only way this would be possible would be for the representative to come from a constituency in which everyone agreed among themselves how to vote on every issue that came before Congress. The worst possible case of representation, where agency loss is 100 percent, would be for the same set of like-minded voters to be represented by someone who voted the opposite of how every voter preferred.

In real life no representative could possibly please all of his constituents on every single issue that came before the legislature since no territorially based district is comprised of a perfectly homogenous group of partisans. So we expect some amount of agency loss or misrepresentation in any representative relationship, but at the same time, we can say a priori that those representatives who are better able to accurately reflect the political positions of their constituents (less agency loss) are preferable to a case in which the elected officials are not able to accurately reflect the views of their constituents (more agency loss).

The accuracy of representation is predicated on two separate but interrelated issues. The first is the personal judgment of the representative. For each vote, she undergoes a decision-making process to come to a conclusion as how to vote. Many different factors will affect this decision-making process including her own ideology, the view of her constituents, her party's stance on the issue, interest group lobbying, etc. The second factor is the one we are most interested in—the impact of the constituency. In order for the elected official to accurately reflect the views of her district, the voters in the district need to send clear signals about their preferences and the representative needs to understand these signals. If she receives an indication from the voters, she then needs to decide how important it is to reflect these views in her voting behavior at the committee level and on the floor of the House. McCrone and Kuklinski argue that in order for the delegate model of representation to work, two conditions must be equally well satisfied.[21] First, elected officials must think of themselves as delegates. This is to say that they must consider constituency opinion to be a major component of their decision-making calculus for voting in Congress. Second, in order for the delegate model to work, voters must send clear and consistent signals to their representatives about how they prefer the representative to vote.

The second factor that affects the cumulative agency loss suffered by a constituency is the ideological makeup of the district itself. This factor is completely out of the hands of an elected official. If the makeup of a district is particularly diverse, then it will necessarily increase the amount of agency loss that voters will experience. If 40 percent of the district prefers to keep minimum wage at its current level and 60 percent of the district prefers a raise in the minimum wage, it is impossible for the elected official to please everyone. If we assume the representative is listening to her constituents (and this is a good assumption to make), then she will vote to increase the minimum wage. Those voters in the minority in this district will not have had their preferences reflected by the voting behavior of their member of Congress.

The point is made more clearly by relying on some simple spatial models, such as those used by Anthony Downs.[22] Imagine a district in which the ideology of the constituents is distributed normally (a bell-shaped distribution). Downs demonstrated that given some simple assumptions, voters will cast their ballots in such a way to minimize the distance between themselves and the elected official, so in an election between two major party candidates we would expect both candidates to converge toward the middle, or the median voter. Candidates place themselves in an ideological position that is going to attract the most votes so that they can win the election. In two-party competition this point turns out to be the median in the distribution. The median has an interesting property—it is the point that minimizes the cumulative deviations. So if you take every element of the distribution, subtract it from the median, take the absolute value, and then add them all up, this number will necessarily be smaller than if any other point in the distribution is used for this same exercise.[23] So the median is where a candidate should locate to attract more votes than his opponent, but this spot in the distribution also minimizes the cumulative amount of agency loss. So inherent electoral dynamics minimize agency loss in a district regardless of what the district looks like. In the quest for votes, candidates naturally move to the middle of the distribution where most of the votes are located.

However, this does not imply that the amount of total distance between the median and all other points is particularly low. For instance compare Figures 2.1 and 2.2—the first one is a distribution with a large degree of

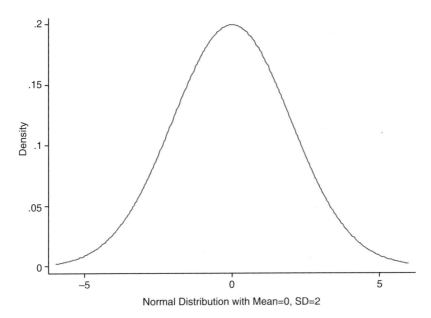

Figure 2.1 Distribution with larger standard deviation.

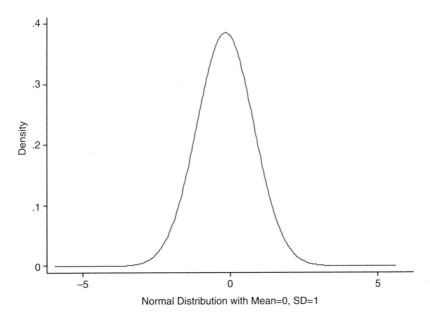

Figure 2.2 Distribution with smaller standard deviation.

variance (or a large standard deviation). The median of this distribution is located at 0 and the standard deviation is 2. The second distribution has the exact same median (at 0) but only has a standard deviation of 1. The elements in the second figure are more tightly crowded around the center of the distribution, while in the first figure there is more diversity in the elements. Note that if the median voter is decisive, the elected official from each of these distributions is exactly the same (located at 0). However, if we measure the amount of satisfaction among the voters, again measured by the cumulative amount of agency loss, it is obvious that the overall level of satisfaction within the second distribution of voters will be much higher than that of the first. Why? Because the distribution is less heterogeneous and the standard deviation is smaller, which means cumulative agency loss will be less. Simply put, most of the voters are located quite close to the elected official on the ideological spectrum.

Thus, from this perspective, the electoral process encourages candidates to represent those views near the center of the distribution of ideology in each electoral district. Rational candidates will locate themselves at or near the center of this distribution regardless of how much variance there is in the distribution. Therefore, it is possible to further maximize representation by minimizing the ideological diversity within each district; the most straightforward way of doing this is to use partisanship in the form of party registration data and election outcome data as a basis for drawing packed districts. Instead of drawing districts to try to increases the odds of having a competitive general election, which necessarily requires a distribution evenly divided between the two parties, we draw districts that are as ideologically homogeneous as possible by putting Democrats with other Democrats, and Republicans with other Republicans to whatever extent is workable.

The composition of a district fundamentally restricts the degree to which a representative can, *from the outset*, accurately reflect the views of the voters in a district. The more ideologically diverse the district, all else being equal, the more agency loss the constituents will suffer. Conversely, the more homogeneous a district, the better able the elected official is to accurately reflect the views of more of his constituents. While the member of Congress from a homogeneous district could still vote in a way that does not reflect the views of the voters in the district (political scientists refer to this as "shirking"), this would be done at the risk of alienating his constituents. All elected officials will naturally try to please some subset of their geographic constituency—obviously one tries to please a sufficient number of would-be voters in order to get reelected (Fenno calls this sub-group the "reelection constituency"[24]).

The important point to take away from this discussion is that the composition of a district is the determining factor as to how well any representative can respond to the voters. The more diverse the district, the less possible it is to reduce agency loss. In this dyadic representational relationship, it is impossible to fully and accurately represent the views of most constituents when the constituents have diametrically opposing points of view. This is not to say that there have not been representatives that have "cross-over appeal" to voters from the other party. Connie Morella was a long time Republican representative from a fairly liberal district in Maryland. In order to keep her seat, she had to vote with the Democrats fairly often. Charlie Stenholm was, until 2006, an old-fashioned southern Democrat, who represented a majority Republican district and got many votes from Republicans in the area. He had to play nice with the Republican Party because most of his constituents were Republicans. The point is that it is harder for anyone to represent a district in which there is a wide variety of opinions on the issues of the day. Imagine the task of one person translating the political preferences of Trent Lott and Edward Kennedy simultaneously! These two gentleman rarely agree on anything, so representing both of these points of view simultaneously is impossible—when one wants X, the other prefers not-X. What is a representative to do? He can either vote for X, vote for not-X, or abstain from voting altogether. None of these alternatives is particularly satisfying for the elected official or the constituents.

Thus, we expect representation to be better, in the sense that more voters will be happy with the behavior of their representative, as ideological homogeneity increases within districts. Representatives cannot be more responsive to their constituents in competitive districts because their districts are too ideologically diverse to represent. One of the main justifications for increasing competitiveness in congressional (or state legislative) elections is that it will increase the responsiveness of our representatives. The closer the election, the more uncertain the member is of getting reelected, and the harder he will have to work to earn the votes from his constituents. While heightened competitiveness does increase uncertainty for elected officials, and will likely increase the amount of time and money an incumbent spends in the district, it does not make the representative a better representative. Indeed, I argue that competitive districts make for worse representation since it is impossible for someone to accurately represent a district with voters who disagree with one another on the major issues facing the country. So if by "responsiveness" we mean having an incumbent make more trips back to the district or spend more time raising money and campaigning, then competitive elections do the trick. If, however, by responsiveness we mean that the member cares about what the constituency thinks, and has the ability to translate those wishes into votes, then competitive elections rather than making representatives more responsive, make them significantly less so.

Two major factors affect how responsive or how representative an elected official will be. The first factor has to do with the ability of a representative to know and respond to the opinions of his constituency. Can he tell how voters in his district want him to vote on the issue of immigration? This factor will vary from person to person. Some representatives might take the delegate approach to representation and not worry so much about the attitudes of the voters in the district, preferring instead to vote in the manner that he decides is best and then relying on his ability to educate and inform the folks back home about why he voted a certain way. Others are keenly interested in and aware of what the voters in the district want and act in a way to please their reelection constituency.

The second factor that affects how well an elected official represents a district is completely exogenous to the process of elections and representation—how much agreement is there among the voters in the district on the important issues of the day? The key point here is that the ideological composition of a district determines, in part, the extent to which voters in the district will be represented in the legislatures. The more unified the voters in the district are, the easier (and more likely) an elected official is to be responsive to the voters. As the diversity of opinions in a district increases, the elected official is less able to translate voter preferences into public policy.

Thus, my goal here is to provide a basis by which we can judge how well a representative represents his constituency. Individuals will be more or less satisfied with their representation conditional on how well their personal preferences get translated into actions by the representative. When a representative does something that a voter does not agree with, the representative has not represented this particular voter very well and the voter experiences agency loss. The cumulative amount of agency loss that a constituency experiences is then a measure of how well (poorly) a representative has translated the preferences of his constituents into action in the legislature. We have elections to encourage representatives to remain faithful to the wishes of the people and the desire to get reelected is the cornerstone of this relationship. Thus, we have properly motivated our representatives to do the best that they can in terms of receiving signals from voters and trying to translate these disparate preferences into behavior in the legislature that maximizes the chances of winning reelection. The second half, and much ignored, part of the equation however, is that some districts are designed in such a way to allow for more people to be represented—those districts that are relatively homogenous—while others are designed in such a way that only a fraction of the population will see their wishes get represented—diverse or competitive districts.

# Chapter 3

# Voters prefer to win elections

## Introduction

This book opened with a story about the post-election blues that Democrats across the country felt after the reelection of President George W. Bush in 2004. This story may be unique insofar as it involved the president of the country, whose election four years prior was effectively decided by the Supreme Court. However, does winning or losing an election at the congressional level have a similar effect on citizens? Are voters measurably more (less) satisfied when their preferred candidate wins (loses) the election? In this chapter I show that the evidence strongly suggests that this is indeed the case. Namely, voters who cast a vote for the candidate who wins the election are systematically happier with their representative, evaluate Congress as an institution more positively, and feel more efficacious than losing voters. The evidence is not likely to surprise anyone as it makes perfect sense—people are happier when they win, be it in a sports competition, on Jeopardy, or voting in an election. But with politics it is not simply the act of one's preferred candidate winning an election that is so satisfactory, but rather the increased likelihood that the voter will be well represented in the federal government and see public policy enacted that is closer to their own ideal point than are the losers. Winners are more likely to have trust in the elected officials and are likely to have expressed stronger senses of satisfaction with the outcome and with democracy in general.

Next, I investigate whether or not the margin of victory in an election affects the attitudes of voters. Going beyond the winner–loser dichotomy perhaps the closeness of the election also has substantive effects on voters' attitudes toward government. For instance, it could be the case that it is much more satisfying to the average voter to win by just a few votes than it is to win in a landslide. The contest was closer; it was not obvious until the election returns came in who was really going to win; along with the feeling of victory is a sense of relief that "my guy won." If you live in a homogeneous district and everyone knows the incumbent is going to win again by 100,000 votes, the winning voter may be happy that his preferred candidate is in office, but is there really anything to savor in that kind of victory? Losers, on the other hand, may feel all the more disappointed if their preferred candidate loses by a handful of votes rather than losing by thousands of votes. So the effect of the margin of victory in the election could differ for winners and losers. The data demonstrate that there are differences for these two groups. Winners systematically drive the positive relationship for the effect of margin of victory on the dependent variables. Losers, on the other hand, are unaffected by the margin of victory. Which is to say, there is no statistically discernible effect of competitive or noncompetitive elections on the attitudes of losing voters. For those readers who do not want to wade through the data in this chapter, the executive summary is as follows: winners are more satisfied than losers, and the degree of competitiveness does not really matter, except in the case of winning voters in which case more uncompetitive elections generally lead to higher degrees of satisfaction. Moreover, the closer the representative is to the voter ideologically, the more satisfied is the voter. Thus, homogenous districts, with as many Democrats or Republicans packed into each district as possible, are going to maximize voter satisfaction and improve representation and attitudes toward government.

## Winners and losers

To say that voters whose preferred candidate wins are more satisfied with the elected representative than voters who cast their vote in favor of the candidate that lost is not going to elicit much dissent. Indeed, the statement is borderline tautological and is more likely to be met with a response such as "Of course!" The point of this chapter is first to make the simple empirical connection between voting for the winning candidate and increased levels of satisfaction and trust, and also to provide the logical basis for a fundamental change in the way that we approach redistricting and competitiveness.

A developing literature suggests that voters' evaluations of government, including overall trust in government, are directly related to whether they cast a ballot for the winning candidate. Anderson and LoTempio show that citizens who voted for the winning presidential candidate have significantly higher levels of overall trust in government relative to voters whose candidate lost the election (even after controlling for other factors that affect trust).[1] Thus, evaluations of the government depend, in part, on election outcomes—voters who feel that their preferences are somehow more represented in the federal government rate the government more highly due to the simple fact that the candidate that they voted for won the election and took office. These voters are more satisfied with the government and they have significantly higher levels of trust in government than losing voters. In this same study Anderson and LoTempio also tested to see if voting for the winner or the loser in the House race affects overall levels of trust in government, but they were not able to find a link. This result, however, is probably due to the fact that when voters are asked about "trust in the federal government," they are far more likely to think about who the president is rather than who their local member of Congress is or which party controls a majority of the seats in Congress.[2]

Clarke and Acock show that voting for the winning candidate in American elections increases voter efficacy as well.[3] They demonstrate that there exists both "outcome contingent" effects and "pure outcome" effects on voters' sense of efficaciousness. Which is to say the outcome contingent effects are those effects on efficacy that are conditional on whether the voter "voted for the winner," while pure outcome effects will be manifest only in nonvoters by increasing their feelings of efficacy because the candidate that they supported, but did not actually vote for, wins the election. Clarke and Acock found that outcome contingent effects are present for American voters in terms of both their vote for the president and their vote for a member of Congress. Interestingly, they also find that neither the act of voting itself nor participation in a political campaign have any effect on efficacy, but voting for the winning candidate does. Moreover, Clarke and Acock do find evidence for pure outcome effects at least at the level of the president; which is to say, if a citizen does not vote but knows that the candidate that he preferred won the election, the voter experiences higher levels of efficacy.[4] This is because the voter feels like his political wishes will be represented in the federal government by the simple fact that the candidate they felt closer to was indeed elected. Thus, people are happier and feel higher levels of political efficacy when the candidates that they support are in fact elected.

There are several other recent examinations of the impact of competitiveness on efficacy in American elections. Brunell and Buchler,[5] and Brunell[6] find that voters that experience competitive elections are not more efficacious than those that live in districts that have landslide elections. In fact, winning voters in landslide districts were more efficacious than winning voters in districts with close election outcomes. For losing voters the margin of victory has no impact. Barreto and Streb find that the relationship between competition and efficacy has changed over time.[7] In the 1960s they find that close elections did correspond with voters feeling more efficacious politically, but by the 1990s and into the twenty-first century that relationship had flipped. Now, voters in competitive districts are less likely to trust in government and less likely to feel like they can really have an impact on politics.

These results are not unique to the American case. Anderson and Guillory demonstrate that a similar winner–loser relationship exists in other advanced industrial democracies.[8] Clarke and Kornberg show that winning voters in Canada have more positive evaluations of their members of parliament in terms of responsiveness to voters. This "winning effect" extends not only to voters, but is also effective at the elite (candidate) level.[9] Bowler and Donovan demonstrate that attitudes of elites toward electoral institutions are, in part, dependent on whether they win the election.[10] Winning candidates, who have been delivered to parliament by the current electoral arrangement, are much more satisfied and committed to these institutions than are losing candidates.

Anderson et al. write "casting one's ballot for a party or a candidate does not automatically turn voters into winners and losers; it is only through the compilation of all voters' choices on the basis of an agreed-upon formula that a president or legislators are elected and a government is thereafter formed, and that the electorate can be subsequently divided into those on the winning and those on the losing side."[11] They go on to say "wins and losses are individually experienced but collectively determined."[12] If we can somehow affect the ratio of winners to losers in a positive fashion, should we do so? After all, it is not the case that voters whose preferred candidate loses are immediately suspect of everything about the government and want to start a revolt. Anderson et al. show that more losers are satisfied with how the government is functioning than the number of losers who are dissatisfied.[13] Moreover, a majority of losers believe that the election in which their candidate lost was, despite the outcome, "fair." I think we should do something to affect the ratio of winners to losers; not only can we substantially reduce the number of people who lose the election, but in doing so, we can actually improve representation and make it virtually impossible for one party to gerrymander the other party out of seats in Congress or in the state legislature.

## Theory and data

The theory driving this investigation is simple: citizens who vote for the winning candidate in a House election will be systematically more likely to have higher evaluations of said candidate relative to voters who vote for the losing candidate. Similarly, "winning" voters will have more positive and fewer negative things to say about their representative and than "losing" voters. Winning voters will be systematically happier with the outcome of the election, be more satisfied with their representative, and be more satisfied with Congress as an institution. Voters whose candidates take public office are likely to see public policy that more closely approximates their own personal points of view than those voters whose candidates lost. Voters want to elect candidates from their own political party. Many political scientists rely on what we call the spatial model of voting in which voters and candidates are placed on a single dimension continuum and voters make their decision about whom to vote for simply by choosing the candidate that is closest to them ideologically. Thus, the closer one's representative is to one's own ideology, the happier is the individual. Indeed, in a perfect world, a representative would act *exactly* as each voter preferred—in that sense a true re-presentation of one's self. Thus, voters cast ballots for the major party candidate that is closest to their own ideological positions (i.e., voters minimize the ideological distance between themselves and the candidate). So when a voter casts a losing ballot, then the distance between the voter and the elected official is necessarily larger. Therefore, the first two hypotheses can be specified:

H1:   Voter satisfaction (efficacy, incumbent approval, etc.) will be higher when the voter is a winner.

H2:   Voter satisfaction will be higher when the ideological distance between the voter and the representative is smaller.

Beyond the simple dichotomy of winning and losing, the margin of victory may also impact voter satisfaction and the other various dependent variables that are utilized here. Common wisdom suggests that as competitiveness goes down (and the margin of victory goes up) voters may be more dissatisfied with the outcome. Winning by a wide margin means that a voter's single ballot is far from decisive and the outcome of the election has very little uncertainty surrounding it. Thus, for both winning and losing voters, their satisfaction and efficacy could conceivably be lower in these instances. However, winning an election by a narrow margin suggests a great deal of uncertainty about the outcome, which would make a victory all the more satisfying. It is possible that the impact of competitiveness could be different for losers than winners. Losing a close election might be significantly more heart-wrenching than having one's candidate win in a landslide. So the slope of the line for the margin of victory could be negative for winners (satisfaction or efficacy might go down as the margin goes up), but for losers the slope could be positive (closer elections lead to less satisfaction because voters are more distraught from the loss). Thus, beyond just examining the effect of the margin of victory on voters *writ large*, the models test whether the margin affects winners and losers differently.

While common wisdom suggests that competitiveness may increase voter satisfaction, my theory implies several things. First, winning and losing is the primal relationship here and the margin by which the election is decided does not have a major effect. There is some evidence from the social psychological literature that suggests that the act of voting itself increases a voter's perception of his preferred candidate's chances of winning. Regan and Kilduff asked two groups of voters about the probability that the candidate that they prefer will win the election.[14] One group consisted of voters *just about to vote*, while the other groups consisted of individuals who *had just finished voting*. The second group of voters was significantly more optimistic about their candidate's chance of prevailing than the first group. Regan and Kilduff attribute this to the fact that "optimism about favorable outcomes is increased when people act on their preferences in significant and irrevocable ways, such as by voting or betting."[15] Thus, voters believe that they will win after they have cast their ballot, even if there is evidence to suggest that they will not. Other research on the same topic demonstrates that the ratio of optimistic voters to pessimistic voters is quite high, even for years in which the election outcome is fairly certain well ahead of time.[16] Thus, the "objective" criteria of competitiveness matters less since voters think that they are going to win.

Second, elections won by very large margins tend to be those from very homogeneous districts.[17] Homogeneous districts contain lots of like-minded individuals who all end up getting a representative that they like (or at the very least the representative is from the political party that they prefer) and therefore incumbent approval ought to be quite high. Put differently, there are going to be lots of winners in homogeneous noncompetitive districts and winning voters are more satisfied and more trusting in government than are losing voters. Therefore, my hypothesis with respect to the margin of victory is that it will be positively related to the various dependent variables in question (efficacy, trust in government, etc.).

> H3:   The margin of victory in the House election will have no effect on voter satisfaction for losing voters and it will be positively related for winning voters.

It is important to distinguish between competitive districts and competitive elections. Competitive districts are those that have been drawn so that there is a rough parity between the two major political parties. But even districts drawn to induce competitive elections do not always work in the intended way. In other words, competitive districts do not always lead to competitive elections. The competitiveness of an election in any district is most highly related to a) whether there is an incumbent present and b) the quality of the challenger.[18] Open-seat elections are generally much more competitive than elections with an incumbent present. When an incumbent is running for reelection, the single variable that is going to increase the odds of having a competitive election is whether or not a high-quality candidate has emerged as a challenger. Of course, the emergence of a good challenger is related to many other variables such as the state of the economy, the reputation of the incumbent, etc. The margin of victory variable tests the effect of a competitive election, but it is not necessarily related to competitive districts. Technically, since my argument centers on redistricting, I am fundamentally interested in the competitiveness of districts, rather than elections. In addition to using the margin of victory as a measure of competition, it is also important to operationalize the notion of a competitive district in the statistical models. Districts drawn to increase the chances of a competitive election (i.e., 50/50 districts) are not necessarily the same districts that actually have competitive elections, thus the need for this variable. The standard approach for quantifying competitive districts is to take the congressional district vote for president in the most recent election and use the closeness of that race as an indicator of district competitiveness. For the same reasons that I expect that competitive elections will be positively related to voter satisfaction, I expect that the competitive district variable will be, if anything, positively related to the host of dependent variables that tap into voter happiness.

> H4:   District competitiveness will be positively related to voter satisfaction.

I tested these four propositions using the American National Election Study (ANES) cumulative file with survey data from 1948–2004 merged with election returns for the House of Representatives going back to 1948. I used a variety of dependent variables to ascertain the nature of the impact of winning–losing and competitiveness on the attitudes of voters.

## Results

First, in order to establish the relationship between voting for the winner and higher degrees of satisfaction, some simple cross-tabulations of the data are suggestive. To examine the relationship between whether a voter was a winner or a loser and that voter's affect toward the representative, the following question from the National Election study is used where respondents are asked the following open-ended question: "Is there anything in particular that you liked about [U.S. House incumbent candidate]? What is that? Anything else?" Respondents are also asked if there is anything that they disliked about the incumbent representative. The survey records up to four responses for both likes and dislikes. Social scientists then can measure affect for a candidate by simply taking the number of likes and subtracting the number of dislikes. So if a voter has four positive and one negative thing to say, then this results in an affect of +3. If a voter has four positive and four negative things to say, then the affect is 0. So this variable ranges from +4 to –4. Table 3.1 presents the results of a cross-tabulation of affect for the incumbent and whether the respondent's candidate won or lost.

There is a clear pattern in the table. Winning voters have very few negative things to say about their representative and quite a few positive things to say, while losers have a significant number of negative responses and far fewer positive things to say than winners. For instance, less than 5 percent of winning voters have a negative score on affect, while 35.6 percent of the losing voters end up with a negative affect score. Similarly, voters for the winning candidate are far more likely to have more positive things to say about their incumbent representative than are losing voters. Over 65 percent of the people that voted for the winner had more positive things to say than negative, while only 23.6 percent of losing voters respond more positively than negatively. This pattern indicates that when people vote for the winner, their affect for their representative is significantly more positive than for losers. The statistical test also supports the hypothesis of a relationship between these two variables at probability p<.001.

Next we investigate whether the winning–losing dichotomy affects voters in a simple way—approval of the incumbent representative. This question does not require voters to think about positive and/or negative aspects about their representative, but rather just whether they approve of the incumbent or not. Table 3.2 displays the results. Only 13.6 percent of winning voters disapproved of the incumbent, while 55.3 percent of losing voters disapproved of

*Table 3.1* Relationship between voting for winning candidate and likes minus dislikes for the incumbent representative

| Incumbent affect (likes–dislikes) | Losing voter | Winning voter | Total |
|---|---|---|---|
| −4 | 63 | 12 | 75 |
|  | 3.1% | 0.2% | 0.8% |
| −3 | 101 | 29 | 130 |
|  | 4.9% | 0.4% | 1.4% |
| −2 | 222 | 87 | 309 |
|  | 10.8% | 1.2% | 3.4% |
| −1 | 348 | 217 | 565 |
|  | 16.8% | 3.1% | 6.2% |
| 0 | 842 | 2,055 | 2,897 |
|  | 40.8% | 29.4% | 32.0% |
| 1 | 221 | 1,618 | 1,839 |
|  | 10.7% | 23.1% | 20.3% |
| 2 | 162 | 1,481 | 1,643 |
|  | 7.8% | 21.2% | 18.1% |
| 3 | 71 | 874 | 945 |
|  | 3.4% | 12.5% | 10.4% |
| 4 | 36 | 629 | 665 |
|  | 1.7% | 9.0% | 7.3% |
| Total | 2,066 | 7,002 | 9,068 |
|  | 100% | 100% | 100% |

Entries represent the number of respondents from the cumulative American National Election Study file 1948–2004 who answered questions about the number of likes and dislikes they have about their incumbent Representative, column percentages below entries. The overall affect is simply the number of likes (up to 4) minus the number of dislikes (up to 4). Chi-squared-(8 df)=1,900, p<.001. Losing voters are those who reported voting for the candidate in the House election that lost, and winning voters are those who reported voting for the winning House candidate.

the incumbent representative. Over 86 percent of winning voters express approval of the elected official while among losers less than 45 percent of these voters approved. These results are not surprising—people who vote for the winning candidate are happier with the elected official than are people who voted for the losing candidate—and they fit well with what is expected based on much of the literature on the subject of how attitudes toward government are conditioned by how people cast their ballots and who wins the election.[19] People are more satisfied with the government (or its component parts) when the candidates that they vote for are elected.

The relationship between winning and losing also moves beyond how a voter feels toward a specific representative. Election outcomes influence the ways in which citizens connect with Congress as an institution. For instance, Table 3.3 is a cross-tabulation of a respondent's overall rating of Congress and whether a voter is a winner or a loser. In the Losing Voter column there are higher percentages of respondents that rate Congress as doing either a "very

*Table 3.2* Relationship between voting for the winning candidate and approval of incumbent

| Approve of House incumbent | Losing voter | Winning voter | Total |
|---|---|---|---|
| Approve | 1,034 | 6,300 | 7,334 |
| | 44.7% | 86.4% | 76.3% |
| Disapprove | 1,281 | 994 | 2,275 |
| | 55.3% | 13.6% | 23.7% |
| Total | 2,315 | 7,294 | 9,609 |
| | 100.0% | 100.0% | 100.0% |

Entries represent the number of respondents from the cumulative American National Election Study file 1948–2004 who either approve or disapprove of the incumbent Representative, column percentages below entries. Chi-squared=1700, p<.001. Losing voters are those who reported voting for the candidate in the House election that lost, and winning voters are those who reported voting for the winning House candidate.

*Table 3.3* Relationship between voting for the winning candidate and approval of Congress

| Performance of Congress rating | Losing voter | Winning voter | Total |
|---|---|---|---|
| Very poor job | 47 | 71 | 118 |
| | 5.7% | 3.9% | 4.4% |
| Poor job | 257 | 494 | 751 |
| | 31.1% | 27.0% | 28.3% |
| Fair job | 414 | 944 | 1,358 |
| | 50.1% | 51.5% | 51.1% |
| Good job | 99 | 300 | 399 |
| | 12.0% | 16.4% | 15.0% |
| Very good job | 9 | 23 | 32 |
| | 1.1% | 1.3% | 1.2% |
| Total | 826 | 1,832 | 2,658 |
| | 100.0% | 100.0% | 100.0% |

Entries represent the number of respondents from the cumulative American National Election Study file 1948–2004 who indicated how they rate the job that Congress is doing, column percentages below entries. Chi-squared (4 df) =15.4, p<.004. In the original dataset there are nine valid responses to the dependent variable, here they have been collapsed. Losing voters are those who reported voting for the candidate in the House election that lost, and winning voters are those who reported voting for the winning House candidate.

poor job" or a "poor job" compared to the respective entries for Winning Voters. The differences are not particularly profound, but they are real and statistically significant. Roughly half of losers and winners rate Congress as doing a "fair job," while more winners have a positive outlook on the national legislature than losers. Some 16.4 percent of winners think Congress is doing a good job, while only 12 percent of losers feel the same way. While the differences shown in this table are more modest than differences shown in earlier tables, they still indicate that it is possible to increase satisfaction with Congress by creating more winners, which is surely a positive development.

Next we turn to a question from the survey that asks respondents how much attention they think their representatives pays to the district that they have been elected to represent. The results seen in Table 3.4 follow the same pattern that emerged in the prior examples. Losing voters are more like to say "not much," while winners tend to say "some" or "a good deal" more often.

We can extract further supportive evidence for the positive relationship between voting for the winning candidate and how the voters evaluates Congress by examining a question from the NES survey that asks the survey respondents which branch of government they trust the most. This question asks respondents to choose among the following four institutions as to a) which one they trust the most and b) which one they trust the least: Congress, the Supreme Court, the president, or political parties. The cross-tabulation of this question and whether the voter is a winner or a loser is presented in Table 3.5. The biggest difference between winners and losers is seen in the percent of respondents who trusted Congress the most. Less than 25 percent of losers picked Congress, while nearly 30 percent of winners chose it as the most trusted institution. Thus, winning voters are much more likely, relative to losing voters, to choose Congress as their most trusted branch of the federal government and they approve of their elected representative more often than losers. The analysis up to this point has been bivariate in nature—where we examine the impact of one variable on another. Clearly, a voter's attitudes

Table 3.4 Relationship between voting for the winning candidate and impression of how much attention MC pays to district

| How much attention incumbent pays to district | Losing voter | Winning voter | Total |
| --- | --- | --- | --- |
| Not much | 265 | 540 | 805 |
|  | 22.1% | 18.5% | 19.5% |
| Some | 690 | 1,742 | 2,432 |
|  | 57.5% | 60.0% | 59.0% |
| A good deal | 246 | 638 | 884 |
|  | 20.5% | 21.9% | 21.5% |
| Total | 1,201 | 2,920 | 4,121 |
|  | 100.0% | 100.0% | 100.0% |

Entries represent the number of respondents from the cumulative American National Election Study file 1948–2004 rating their member of Congress in terms of the amount of attention respondent feels that incumbent pays to district, column percentages below entries. Chi-squared=15.35, p<.004. Losing voters are those who reported voting for the candidate in the House election that lost, and winning voters are those who reported voting for the winning House candidate.

*Table 3.5* Relationship between voting for the winning candidate and which branch of government a citizen trusts the most

| Branch respondent trusts the most | Losing voter | Winning voter | Total |
|---|---|---|---|
| Congress | 139 | 343 | 482 |
| | 24.6% | 29.7% | 28.0% |
| Supreme Court | 256 | 513 | 769 |
| | 45.2% | 44.3% | 44.6% |
| President | 157 | 281 | 438 |
| | 27.7% | 24.3% | 25.4% |
| Political parties | 14 | 20 | 34 |
| | 2.5% | 1.7% | 2.0% |
| Total | 566 | 1,157 | 1,723 |
| | 100.0% | 100.0% | 100.0% |

Entries represent the number of respondents from the cumulative American National Election Study file 1948–2004 who choose each branch of the federal government that "they trust the most," column percentages below entries. Chi-squared (3 df)=6.43, p<.09. Losing voters are those who reported voting for the candidate in the House election that lost, and winning voters are those who reported voting for the winning House candidate.

toward a representative or toward Congress as a whole are going to be dependent on a whole host of different variables. So in order to more fully understand the relationship between winning and losing, the margin of victory, and ideological distance between the voter and the representative, we also need to conduct some multivariate analyses to see how each of these variables (and some control variables) affect voters' attitudes toward government simultaneously.

Tables 3.6 and 3.7 present the results of the multivariate analysis. There are four separate dependent variables based on questions from the election surveys. The first variable is one in which survey respondents are asked about their approval of the incumbent member of Congress. The variable takes on two values: 1 if the respondent approves of the job the incumbent member of Congress is doing, and 0 if the respondent does not approve. The variables of interest include margin of victory, which is the absolute value of the difference between the Democrat and Republican share of the vote in each respective congressional district. The vote for loser variable indicates whether the person voted for the losing candidate or not (losers are coded 1, winners and non-voters are coded 0). The nonvoter variable indicates whether the survey respondent reported having voted in the election or not (1 for nonvoter, 0 for voter). The presidential margin of victory is intended to capture the difference between competitive *elections* and competitive *districts*. This number is calculated the same way that the congressional margin of victory is, except the data are from the most recent presidential election results from the district. This is a more objective measure of the underlying degree of competitiveness in a district since even a district drawn to induce competitive elections may not do so every year. Since many House elections happen without any real opponent for the incumbent there is a variable to control for these elections as well. If an election is uncontested, this variable takes on a value of 1 and is 0 otherwise. Finally, to control for the electoral power of incumbency, a variable indicating whether or not an incumbent ran in the election in question is also included (1 = incumbent present, 0 = open seat).

As mentioned above, there is a variable included in the model to capture the ideological distance between the voter and the candidate. Respondents are asked, in this survey, to place themselves on a seven-point ideological scale and they are asked to place the Democratic and Republican candidates running for the House on the same scale. Thus, it is possible to measure the distance that the voter perceives there to be between himself and the candidates that are running for the seat. We take the difference between the voter and the eventual winner and square it so that larger distances between the two points are exaggerated. Each model is run twice—once with the ideological distance squared variable included and once without this variable. This is done because a significant proportion of the survey respondents do not answer the questions that place the candidates on the seven-point scale. When this variable is included, the sample size for the model is significantly smaller than when the variable is dropped. Since the number of respondents drops so significantly when this variable is in the equation, it is hypothetically possible that the results are biased. Due to this possibility, models both with and without the ideological distance measure are reported.

There are also a whole host of control variables in the model including age, gender, education, party identification, co-partisan dummy variable, a strength of partisanship variable, and questions about how people felt about the state of the national economy and their personal financial situation. These variables may also affect a respondent's disposition toward government or a specific representative, so they must be included in the equation so that we come closer to isolating the effects of being a winner or experiencing a competitive election.

Voter attitudes toward the incumbent representative are examined first. The first two columns of Table 3.6 present the results of the analyses for approval of the incumbent. The first model excludes the ideological distance variable, and the second one includes it. One can see how dramatically this variable affects the number of respondents in the sample size for the model—there are more than twice as many without it (11,541), relative to when it is included (5,181).

The coefficient for margin of victory variable in both of these models is positive and significant. This indicates that as the election become more *uncompetitive* (the margin is greater), the more likely the respondent is to have *positive* feelings of approval toward the incumbent representative. While this is not necessarily a causal relationship—a voter is simply less satisfied just because

*Table 3.6* The impact of competitiveness on measures of satisfaction with the incumbent and Congress

| Variable | Approve of incumbent | | Incumbent affect | |
|---|---|---|---|---|
| Margin of victory | **1.93** | **2.65** | **1.248** | **2.00** |
| | (6.23) | (5.63) | (5.12) | (5.11) |
| Vote for loser | **−1.42** | **−1.282** | **−1.388** | **−1.477** |
| | (22.53) | (14.52) | (23.90) | (16.46) |
| Nonvoter | **−0.592** | **−0.463** | **−0.641** | **−0.573** |
| | (13.39) | (7.12) | (18.95) | (10.81) |
| Presidential margin of victory | −0.328 | −0.318 | **−0.522** | −0.581 |
| | (1.13) | (0.72) | (2.21) | (1.57) |
| Uncontested | **−0.651** | **−0.842** | **−0.428** | **−0.608** |
| | (5.56) | (4.84) | (4.59) | (4.17) |
| Ideological distance squared | | **−0.062** | | **−0.054** |
| | | (12.63) | | (9.30) |
| Co-partisan dummy | **0.150** | 0.011 | **0.214** | **0.156** |
| | (3.81) | (0.18) | (6.98) | (3.06) |
| Strength of partisanship | −0.03 | 0.012 | **0.032** | 0.05 |
| | (1.66) | (0.40) | (2.10) | (1.86) |
| Age | **0.003** | **0.007** | **0.012** | **0.013** |
| | (3.04) | (3.82) | (13.06) | (9.10) |
| Gender | **−0.110** | −0.081 | −0.027 | −0.074 |
| | (3.23) | (1.57) | (1.02) | (1.70) |
| Education | **−0.035** | −0.006 | 0.018 | 0.015 |
| | (3.13) | (0.34) | (1.91) | (0.92) |
| National economy | **0.090** | 0.057 | 0.022 | 0.029 |
| | (3.58) | (1.54) | (1.10) | (0.91) |
| Pocketbook economy | 0.045 | 0.035 | 0.006 | 0.025 |
| | (1.94) | (1.11) | (0.37) | (0.88) |
| Constant | **1.14** | **0.95** | **0.248** | **0.320** |
| | (9.94) | (5.34) | (2.71) | (2.19) |
| Number of respondents | 11,541 | 5,181 | 11,727 | 4,782 |
| Number of sampling units | 1,644 | 1,111 | 1,565 | 1,000 |

* Entries are unstandardized coefficients with standard errors in parentheses. All models use standard errors clustered on the state, district, and election year. Sampling unit is congressional district/year. Data are from the American National Election Study Cumulative File 1948–2004. Bold entries are statistically significant at $p<.05$ or better. Incumbent approval is dichotomous: 0= don't approve, 1=approve; Incumbent affect is the number of likes (up to four) minus the number of dislikes (up to four) with respect to the incumbent Representative.

the race was closer—it is related to the causal mechanism. As a congressional district becomes less diverse (more political homogeneous), it also becomes less electorally competitive,[20] which means that there are necessarily fewer voters further away from the incumbent in terms of ideology. The analysis was rerun separately for winners and losers and this positive effect of the margin of victory is definitely more powerful for winning voters than losing voters. The coefficient was positive and significant for winners, and positive but not statistically significant for losers.

Both losing voters and nonvoters are less happy with the incumbent relative to winning voters. Since there are dummy variables for nonvoters and losers, the reference category is winning voters. So the negative coefficient for non-voters and for losers indicates that both of these groups are significantly less likely to approve of the incumbent than are winning voters. The coefficients differ in size slightly in the first two models, but not by much and they all are negative and highly significant.

The presidential margin of victory variable, which is intended to capture the underlying competitiveness of the district, is negative but not significant in either model of approval of the incumbent. So voters in districts that have an underlying competitive component, and thus are more likely to have competitive congressional elections in the future, are no more or less likely to approve of the incumbent than voters living in perfectly lopsided districts.

Uncontested elections have negative coefficients for both models and the results are significant. The straightforward interpretation of this result is that voters do not mind less competition, but a complete absence of competition may affect voters negatively. While it is impossible to tell with certainty, there may be another data-related explanation for this result. Recall that the model includes this variable in addition to a margin of victory variable. There might be a "ceiling effect" to the representational benefits of a large margin of victory, which is to say that winning with 80 percent of the vote is no different than winning with 100 percent of the vote. Having a negative coefficient for the uncontested variable will correct for the fact that a linear model assumes that the effect is the same as the difference between a 60 percent vote share and an 80 percent vote share. So, we should not necessarily interpret this to mean that voters dislike uncontested elections, although we cannot reject the possibility.

The ideological distance squared variable is negative and significant as expected. Naturally, the greater the perceived distance between a citizen and her representative, the less likely she is to approve of the incumbent, all else being equal. The co-partisan dummy variable is positive and significant as expected. Beyond that, some of the control variables do significantly impact the dependent variable. For instance, old people are more likely to approve of the incumbent than are young people, on average. The more highly educated a person, the less likely they will approve of the incumbent. The more highly a respondent rates the state of the nation's economy or the state of her own personal financial situation, the more likely she is to give the incumbent a higher rating. Males (gender variable is coded 0=female, 1=male) are less approving of the incumbent on average than are females. Some of the control variables that are significant in the first model are not statistically significant in the second. This is because of the inclusion of the ideological distance squared variable, which is very significant in explaining approval on its own and the sample size is significantly smaller.

This first cut at the data suggests that competition does not increase satisfaction with the representative from the perspective of the individual voter. What is important though is the winner–loser dichotomy. Losers are far less likely to approve of the incumbent than are winners. While Anderson and LoTempio did not find any effect for losers being less trusting in government based on whether their preferred House candidate won or lost, their dependent variable is tapping into attitudes at a more abstract level.[21] Which is to say that they are interested in trust in government, which is much more likely to be affected by votes for the president. How much someone "trusts the federal government" is going to be much more related to who won the presidential election and much less related to who won the House race in their district.

For the next model, the dependent variable is the measure of incumbent affect. Recall from above that this variable is calculated by subtracting the number of dislikes from the number of likes in the survey. Here, like in the previous model, as the election in the district becomes *less competitive*, the *more likely* the voter is to have more good things than negative things to say about the incumbent.

Again both losing voters and nonvoters are significantly less positive toward the member than are winning voters. The coefficient on the loser variable is larger than the nonvoter value, indicating that losers are even less satisfied than are nonvoters, which is not unexpected since the person that they supported lost the election. The presidential margin of victory variable is negative in both models, but only significant in the model that excludes the ideological distance variable. So here there is some indication that as districts become less competitive there is a reduction in the affect for the incumbent. This is counterbalanced, of course, by the results for the margin of victory at the congressional election level. The ideological distance variable has a negative coefficient and is significant, as in the previous model. The co-partisan variable is positive and significant in both models. Besides age, none of the other control variables are significant in these models. Again, having one's preferred candidate is clearly the prime mover when it comes to explaining whether a citizen is going to have a positive or negative evaluation of the candidate. Losing a very close election is not better than winning one by a landslide. Voters want to win and when they do, they are systematically more satisfied with the outcome and with the representative. Next, we focus on how these variables affect voters' attitudes toward Congress as an institution, as well as individual level feelings of political efficacy.

Table 3.7 compiles the results of the analyses for the next two variables. The first variable is from a simple question about whether survey respondents approve of Congress or not. There are three possible values to the variable: a 0 indicates the respondent does not approve of Congress, a 1 indicates the respondent has mixed views of Congress or does not know how to respond, and a 2 means the respondent approves of the legislature. The results of the analysis support the underlying theory regarding representation and competition. Specifically, the margin of victory coefficients for both models of

*Table 3.7* The impact of competitiveness on approval of Congress and efficaciousness

| Variable | Approve of Congress | | Efficacy | |
|---|---|---|---|---|
| Margin of victory | 0.221 | 0.116 | −0.302 | −0.250 |
| | (1.45) | (0.46) | (1.13) | (0.70) |
| Vote for loser | **−0.146** | −0.093 | −0.047 | **−0.134** |
| | (4.70) | (1.79) | (1.19) | (1.93) |
| Nonvoter | 0.026 | 0.056 | **−0.476** | **−0.357** |
| | (1.16) | (1.42) | (15.22) | (6.30) |
| Presidential margin of victory | 0.166 | 0.241 | 0.342 | 0.292 |
| | (1.10) | (0.97) | (1.39) | (0.80) |
| Incumbent dummy | 0.035 | 0.066 | 0.036 | 0.085 |
| | (0.87) | (0.93) | (0.53) | (1.01) |
| Uncontested | −0.058 | −0.092 | 0.139 | 0.136 |
| | (0.98) | (0.93) | (1.43) | (0.98) |
| Ideological distance squared | | **−0.014** | | −0.002 |
| | | (3.83) | | (0.41) |
| Co-partisan dummy | −0.031 | **−0.092** | −0.056 | **−0.137** |
| | (1.38) | (2.33) | (1.91) | (2.63) |
| Strength of partisanship | **0.056** | **0.080** | **0.119** | **0.142** |
| | (5.70) | (4.38) | (8.97) | (6.01) |
| Age | **−0.007** | **−0.007** | **−0.006** | **−0.007** |
| | (11.63) | (6.56) | (7.88) | (5.26) |
| Gender | **−0.174** | **−0.172** | −0.030 | −0.053 |
| | (9.78) | (5.73) | (1.27) | (1.26) |
| Education | **−0.043** | **−0.052** | **0.191** | **0.198** |
| | (6.85) | (4.66) | (23.32) | (13.56) |
| National economy | **0.122** | **0.101** | **0.088** | 0.049 |
| | (9.23) | (4.70) | (4.55) | (1.72) |
| Pocketbook economy | **0.075** | **0.089** | **0.103** | **0.147** |
| | (6.42) | (4.58) | (6.63) | (5.31) |
| Constant | −0.112 | −0.02 | **1.024** | **0.83** |
| | (1.59) | (0.17) | (10.05) | (5.30) |
| Number of respondents | 18,648 | 6,339 | 17,632 | 5,789 |
| Number of sampling units | 2,380 | 1,271 | 2,343 | 1,246 |

* Entries are unstandardized coefficients with standard errors in parentheses. All models use standard errors clustered on the state, district, and election year. Data are from the American National Election Study Cumulative File 1948–2004. Bold entries are statistically significant at $p<.05$ or better. Dependent variables are measured as follows: The dependent variables are as follows: Congressional approval is 0= don't approve, 1=DK or mixed, 2=approve; efficacy was transformed from 0, 25, 50, 75, 100 (standard NES version) to 0, 1, 2, 3, 4, with higher scores indicating more efficaciousness;

congressional approval are positive but fail to reach statistically significant levels. When the analyses are run separately for winners and losers, the coefficient for victory margin is positive and borderline significant for winning voters, and negative but not significant for losers. The vote for loser coefficient is negative in both models, statistically significant in the first and borderline significant in the second (just below the .05 standard). Here the model taps into feelings among citizens toward the whole institution that is Congress rather than about their particular representative, and, again, we see that losing matters whereas how competitive the election was in the district has no impact.

Other variables impact one's feelings toward the national legislature. The ideological distance between oneself and one's representative has a negative impact—which is to say that the bigger the perceived difference, the less satisfied the citizen. The strength of one's partisanship has a positive impact—the more strongly a citizen feels about belonging to one of the two major parties, the more likely that person is, on average, to have a more positive view of Congress. Older citizens tend to have less positive evaluations than younger citizens. Men and highly educated citizens are also less likely to rate Congress high in terms of approval. Finally, a respondent's perceptions regarding the health of the economy as a whole and how well the respondent feels he or she is personally doing economically, both positively affect their evaluations of Congress.

Winning and losing matters with respect to attitudes toward individual members as well as attitudes toward the institution as a whole. Competitiveness bears no impact on these attitudes. One might speculate that voters who experience narrow elections might feel more satisfied toward Congress because of the near decisiveness of their vote, or because the candidates anticipated the closeness of the race and ran better campaigns and the incumbent was more responsive to her constituents. None of these bits of common wisdom are correct. The important variable here is whether or not the representative represents the interests of the individual voter.

The last variable of interest is political efficacy, which is a sense that one's vote matters or that the government cares about what regular citizens think. Low feelings of efficaciousness are associated with disenchanted voters or with people that feel that the government simply represents other people. Obviously whether a voter is a winner or a loser is likely to have some impact on efficaciousness. We also would expect competitiveness to matter here more than any other variable because a component of efficacy is this notion that one's vote really does matter and if the congressional election is particularly lopsided then this could affect how one responds with respect to their own levels of efficacy.[22] However, the coefficients for this variable in both models are equal to zero in a statistical sense. They are negative and when the models are rerun, separating winners from losers, the coefficients are negative for both, but again they do not approach standard levels of significance.

Losers and nonvoters are less efficacious than voters whose preferred candidate wins. This makes good sense insofar as the single-member district system freezes out losing voters by wasting their votes. Nonvoters probably do not vote in part because they do not think voting makes a difference. In this model the ideological distance variable does not matter and the co-partisan variable is actually negative, indicating that if the representative and the respondent are from the same party, the voter tends to be less efficacious than if they were from different parties. People who feel closely allied with a party have higher feelings of efficacy on average, as do more highly educated citizens. The older one gets, the less efficacious one feels on average.

Electoral competition does not affect voters in the ways in which most informed observers expect. To be fair, most calls for election reform and increased competitiveness are more concerned with representation and governance than they are with attitudes toward government among voters, but nonetheless this is an important finding. All of the four hypotheses are generally supported by the data analysis. Winning or losing is the primal factor affecting attitudes toward a voter's specific representative, as well as a major factor in how voters feel toward Congress as an institution and feelings of political efficacy. The margin of victory of a congressional election does not impact losing voters attitudes or feelings toward government—quite simply they are unaffected by whether the election was decided by one vote or 100,000 votes. For winning voters, the results are even more interesting—the less competitive the election, the more likely a voter is to evaluate the representative highly. Homogeneous districts lead to noncompetitive elections, but they also lead to well-represented citizens who are satisfied with their member of Congress and with Congress as an institution.

## Implications

The data analyses demonstrate that winning voters are much more satisfied with their representative than losing voters, and they are more satisfied with Congress as an institution. While this is an interesting and counter-intuitive finding, what, if anything, can we do with this information in terms of real public policy? I argue that the clear implication for redistricting is that states ought to stop drawing districts designed to increase the odds of a competitive election because this approach necessarily maximizes the proportion of voters on the losing side. One of the major liabilities of a single-member district system, like the one for the House of Representatives, is that many votes are "wasted." Wasted votes include every vote for the losing candidate in a House election. In a proportional system virtually no votes are wasted because seats are allocated in the legislature in accordance with the percentage of votes that the party gets in the electorate. So even if a voter's party does particularly badly in one election, that party will still get seats in the legislature, whereas in the current American system a vote for the losing candidate translates into nothing. By purposefully drawing districts that have roughly equal numbers of Democrats and Republicans, the major liability of the single-member district system is exacerbated. Moreover, it is obvious that the margin of victory is not negatively correlated with voters attitudes toward government. Indeed, if anything, the variables are positively correlated. Common wisdom suggests that voters might be more disaffected when the race is strictly uncompetitive, but in this case common wisdom is dead wrong.

Congressional districts are necessarily artificial constructs, so they can be manipulated in many different ways. Here I make the case that districts should be drawn to maximize the number of Democrats or Republicans in a single district. Rather than drawing 50–50 competitive districts, we should draw districts more on the order of 80–20 or even 90–10 in favor of one party or the other. This reduces the number of voters who will vote for the losing candidate, which reduces the number of wasted votes.

There are clearly reasons to draw districts in such a manner as to increase efficacy and happiness with our government, particularly since Congress almost always has significantly lower approval ratings than the president, the Supreme Court, and state governments.[23] Packing districts with like-minded partisans makes a great deal of sense, as long as both major political parties are packed to similar degrees. Drawing competitive districts or systematically "cracking"[24] one party or the other is not beneficial and ought not be present in redistricting plans. Thus, what we think of typically as competitive districts (those with roughly equal numbers of Democrats and Republicans) provide negligible benefits and come with significant costs. One of the most significant benefits from drawing a legislative map with packed districts is that it makes it significantly more difficult to effect a map that constitutes a partisan gerrymander. Districting plans that dilute one party's vote must use a combination of packing and cracking to create a map that contains significant levels of partisan bias (i.e., where one party might win the statewide vote for the House, but still end up with fewer seats).

Preserving communities of interest is one of the main principles guiding map makers. Among these principles, preserving communities of interest is certainly the most ephemeral. What really constitutes a community of interest? Is any American city or county really a community of interest? Sometimes— depending on the issue. A city is a unified community of interest when the issue is nonpartisan; for example, if the issue is the obtainment of federal funds to repair bridges and roads, but it is not if the issue involves anything with ideological disagreement. Properly conceived, I argue, communities of interest should be composed entirely of either Democrats or Republicans (liberals or conservatives) in reflection of the primary cleavage in American politics.[25] On controversial issues, ideological communities of interest will typically face issues in unison, increasing the likelihood that their representative will vote on legislation in Congress in congruence with the vast majority of their constituents. Citizens living in knife-edged districts cannot expect this kind of representation. Drawing districts to increase competitiveness in the general election only optimizes the number of voters that will be upset with their representation. Thus, not only do competitive districts not provide a social "good," but they also actually increase dissatisfaction and make it less likely that voters' preferences are represented in government.

Drawing competitive districts also increases the volatility of the electoral system. If every district is a "50–50" district, then any small change in the voting behavior of the electorate could produce enormous changes in the partisan distribution of seats. While it is true, and often cited, that the founders intended for the House to most closely mirror the wishes of the public, it is not reasonable to assume that they expected the institution to be hyper-sensitive to relatively small changes in the partisan leanings of the people. Districting this way also delivers a disproportionate share of the voting power to independents and moderate swing voters.[26] If a districting plans packs voters from both major parties equally into districts (i.e., the average district is either 80 percent Republican or 80 percent Democratic), this has the added benefit of sending congressional delegations to the House that closely mirror the overall distribution of partisans in that state. A plan with many competitive districts can easily send a delegation to the House that is truly unreflective of the underlying partisan divisions in a state.

Some states, such as Arizona,[27] have passed laws or referenda specifying that a districting plan ought to maximize the number of competitive districts. This is not particularly surprising since the common wisdom among most voters and certainly among the media is that the House of Representatives has far too few competitive districts and that an increase in the number of competitive elections or in the amount of turnover in Congress will somehow enhance representation. There is absolutely no evidence that this is the case.[28] In fact, maximizing the number or proportion of competitive districts is harmful rather than beneficial in many respects. The most obvious effect of drawing cracked or competitive districts is to maximize the number of voters who are dissatisfied with their representation.[29] Second, in a state that draws all or most of its districts in this knife-edged fashion, the likelihood that small swings in voting behavior translates into large swings in the percentage of seats that one party can win in a single election is increased. This can result in statewide representation that is widely incongruent with statewide partisanship, which, in turn, leads to voting behavior in the legislature that does not accurately represent the views of the constituents.

## Conclusion

In this chapter I demonstrated that there are significant and important differences in the attitudes of voters regarding Congress and its members, contingent upon whether the voter's preferred candidate wins or loses the election. Winners are happier with their own representative and with Congress as an institution when they vote for the winning candidate. Even more importantly, the data demonstrate that the margin by which a candidate wins or loses does not have the expected negative effect on voters. It is reasonable to hypothesize that as the margin of victory decreases across districts we would expect the incumbent member of Congress to pay more attention to the constituency—lavishing them with attention and pork barrel projects—to get the requisite number of votes to hang on to the seat. However, the data show, if anything, the larger the margin of victory, the happier is the average voter with the job that the incumbent is doing. How can this be? I suspect it is because competitive districts are diverse districts with nearly as many losing voters as there are winning voters. Thus, as the margin of victory goes up, the average level of satisfaction may also go up since there are so many more winners than losers.

Since there are big differences between winners and losers and, if anything, the bigger the margin of victory the more satisfied are the voters, why not pack districts with like-minded partisans? We can turn more losers into winners and have a great proportion of voters represented by someone who they feel truly represents their interests in the federal government. This approach runs counter to virtually every other suggested reform of redistricting. Most folks agree that it is more competition, not less, that is truly needed in our electoral system. As an example, Fiorina in his popular book about the myth of the existence of a culture war in America does see the current lack of competitiveness in congressional elections as a big problem and one that ought to be fixed. Fiorina, like thousands of other people interested in American politics, bemoans the lack of competition in House elections.[30] "In 2000, when the presidential race was a cliff-hanger, only 74 of the 435 House seats were won by margins less than 55 percent. In 2004, another close presidential election, but after the decennial reapportionment and redistricting cycle, the number of such competitive districts fell to 24."[31] He goes on to advocate that districts in the House of Representatives be drawn to maximize competitiveness, in part because "Independents hold the balance in all districts, providing an incentive for the candidates to appeal to the middle."[32] Fiorina assumes that districts drawn to increase the likelihood of competitive elections will necessarily force candidates toward the center. This assumption is almost certainly wrong. Both Huntington[33] and Fiorina[34] himself, in some earlier work, make a convincing case that the more narrow the majority in a district, the more likely the representative will be more conservative or liberal. Instead of trying to fashion a winning majority out of Independents and moderate Democrats and Republicans, a representative is more likely to stick to his or her guns solidly on the right or the left. Doing the former leaves a representative constantly trying to play both sides of the aisle—trying to please both voters that lean to the left and those that lean to the right. This is not an easy position to be in to be sure.

In the next chapter I turn to the traditional principles that shape the redistricting process. There are some traditional and legal elements that constrain how districts are drawn. The principles are explained and put into context for a typical redistricting and I also examine the extent to which a fair, packed partisan plan is workable under these conditions.

Chapter 4

# Traditional redistricting principles

## Introduction

While there are federal laws and U.S. Supreme Court rulings that widely affect how redistricting is done, ultimately this process is handled at the state government level across the country. For most states the process by which new maps are put into effect is by passing a law. Both chambers of the state legislature and the governor must agree on a new map.[1] Naturally, this process is highly partisan and is rarely completed without significant political conflict. However, given the inherently political aspects of this process, some states have tried to take the politicians out of the process by giving the job to another body, typically an unelected commission. Seven states (Arizona, Hawaii, Idaho, Indiana, Montana, New Jersey, and Washington) use commissions to draw districts for the U.S. House of Representatives. Twelve states (Alaska, Arizona, Arkansas, Colorado, Hawaii, Idaho, Missouri, Montana, New Jersey, Ohio, Pennsylvania, and Washington) use commissions as the primary institution to draw state legislative boundaries. Three more states (Iowa, Maine, and Vermont) have commissions that serve the state government in an advisory capacity to help redistrict.[2] In terms of timing, redistricting is typically done once a decade shortly after the official release of the data from the most recent census. There is no restriction barring states from redistricting more often however. The recent Texas redistricting case that reached the U.S. Supreme Court demonstrated that the Court sees nothing in the Constitution or federal law that prohibits a state from redrawing district lines more than once in any single decade.

This chapter reviews the generally accepted principles that guide how new electoral maps are drawn—principles such as contiguous districts, equal population, preserving communities of interest, preserving political subdivisions, protecting incumbents, and compactness of districts. Some of these principles are more important than others and there are some natural tensions among these competing goals as well. For instance, if we insist that districts have to be equally populated down to the person, then it is much more difficult to preserve political subdivisions, such as cities or counties. There are very few strict parameters that affect how these maps are drawn—the districts do have to be single-member districts and the district must be contiguous. Beyond that many of the "principles" that we associate with redistricting are often ignored by legislators and judges. As each of these principles is reviewed, I also explain what impact, if any, my suggested approach to redistricting has on each one of these principles.

## Single-member districts

Both the methods of and principles guiding redistricting have evolved greatly over time. The House of Representatives was designed to represent the people of each state, thus there is a provision in the Constitution to conduct a census of the population every ten years. The purpose of the census was to reallocate seats in the House *among* the various states in the country. It is worth noting that the Constitution does not specify that each state must utilize single-member districts (SMD) for the House of Representatives and many states did elect representatives from at-large, multi-member districts for many years. The first time that federal law required using single-member districts was when the Apportionment Act of 1842 was signed into law.

Until the early part of the twentieth century, after each decennial census Congress would pass an apportionment bill that would set the overall size of the House of Representatives. The Constitution specified that the each state should have a seat in the House for every 30,000 residents counted in the census. Every state was entitled to at least one seat in the chamber, and the initial size of the House was set at 65 members. This number quickly grew to 240 after the 1830 census. The number of seats in the House grew every decade until 1911 when the size was fixed at 433 with a provision for the addition of one seat each for Arizona and New Mexico when they became States (U.S. Statutes at Large, 37 Stat 13, 14 (1911)). The House has remained at 435 seats save a temporary increase to 437 when Alaska and Hawaii were admitted as states. These decadal apportionment bills were silent as to the exact methods by which members should be elected until 1842.[3] That law stated that representatives "should be elected by districts composed of contiguous territory equal in number to the number of representatives to which said state may be entitled, no one district elected more than one representative." The major problem with not having districts is that in an "at-large" election the arithmetic majority can easily win 100 percent of the seats. In an at-large system every voter gets as many votes as there are seats to fill. If all of the majority party votes cohesively, they can easily win every seat. The move to a single-member district system constituted a move toward more proportionality. However, the use of at-large districts continued to be a problem well into the twentieth century.

Despite the passage of a federal law requiring single-member districts, four states continued to elect members to the House from at-large districts:

Georgia, Mississippi, Missouri, and New Hampshire.[4] All of the officials, elected in illegal at-large districts, were seated in the House of Representatives. In the next apportionment bill, passed in 1850, the SMD requirement was dropped. Ten years later the requirement was reinserted into the bill and signed into law. Until a permanent law was passed in 1929, Congress would pass apportionment bills after each census (except for the 1920 census) and include various requirements about redistricting in the language. For instance, in 1872 they added language so that each district in a state should contain "as nearly practicable an equal number of inhabitants." In 1901 Congress added language concerning the shape of districts by requiring that electoral boundaries be comprised of "compact territory." Many states ignored some or all of these districting provisions. Compliance was such a problem because there was no enforcement of these provisions. Several times the House seated members elected from illegal at-large districts—it is hard to imagine why anyone would bother to comply with the law.

Lani Guinier is a well-known critic of the single-member district system. Guinier and I are on the same page with respect to the use of geography as one of the central principles for drawing districts. We both argue that this is often harmful rather than beneficial for representation. She writes:

> Winner-take-all territorial districting imperfectly distributes representation based on group attributes and disproportionately rewards those who win the representational lottery. Territorial districting uses an aggregating rule that inevitably groups people by virtue of some set of externally observed characteristics such as geographic proximity or racial identity. In addition, the winner-take-all principle inevitably wastes some votes. The dominant group within the district gets all the power; the votes of supporters of nondominant groups of disaffected voters within the dominant group are wasted. Their votes lose significance because they are consistently cast for political losers.[5]
>
> (Guinier 1993)

Where Guinier and I depart company is the necessity of wasting votes in a single-member district system. I advocate that we minimize the number of wasted votes, which makes her distinction between dominant and non-dominant groups less important as the nondominant group is redrawn from several districts into their own district in which they are dominant and a new nondominant group is not created! Her underlying concern is identical to mine—"votes lose significance because they are consistently cast for political loser."

## Equal population

In modern redistricting the principle of one person one vote is virtually sacrosanct. Variance in the population across districts within a state seems unfair on its face. This perception has not always been the case in American redistricting however. Historically, the size of congressional and state legislative districts has varied within a state. Typically, rural districts would be significantly smaller in population than the growing urban districts. In 1960, California had the biggest population discrepancies because the smallest state Senate district had just 15,000 people in it, while the largest district included the entire county of Los Angeles with over six million inhabitants. The ratio of the largest to smallest was over 400. At this time it took a mere 11 percent of the population of the state to elect a majority in the state legislature. Vermont's state constitution guaranteed each town a seat in the lower chamber of the state house, so Stratton with its 24 residents had a single representative as did the city of Burlington which had 35,531 residents—1,480 times as many people. As of 1960, in every single chamber in every single state across the country there was a disparity of *at least* two to one in terms of the ratio of the largest district to the smallest district.

It was the inherent unfairness in these widely differently sized districts that finally forced the Supreme Court to jump into the "political thicket" of redistricting. The first of a series of important cases in the early 1960s was *Baker v. Carr*. This case originated in Tennessee and was brought to the Court because the mayor of Millington, a growing suburban city near Memphis, thought it was impossible to get anything from the state government because of the lack of representation for nonrural areas. The suit was brought under the Equal Protection Clause of the 14th amendment to the Constitution and the argument was that the rights of some of the citizens to equal protection were violated because their votes mattered less in the state government than some of their fellow citizens that resided in districts with fewer people. The main hurdle to overcome in this case was simply the willingness of the Court to agree that the case was justiciable—meaning the Court has the capability of deciding a case in the first place. Nearly twenty years earlier the Court heard a redistricting case and ruled that the issue was not justiciable (*Colegrove v. Green* (1946)). The Court decided that *Baker v. Carr* was justiciable and the Court had jurisdiction over the issue. The case was then remanded back to the lower Court from which it had been sent so that the decision could be altered in the face of this new decision. The significance of the *Baker* case is hard to understate as cases were filed, based on this decision, in at least 34 states around the country within the next year.[6]

Next, the Court decided a case that involved the upper chamber of the Alabama state legislature. In the *Reynolds v. Sims* (1964) decision the Court ruled that both chambers of state legislatures must be apportioned based on population. The structures of American state governments tend to be very similar to that of the federal government. Since the federal government had a bicameral legislature and the upper chamber represents a geographic unit, each state gets equal representation, many state governments designed analogous upper chambers in which, in many cases, counties were equally represented in the chamber. The U.S. Senate is the single most malapportioned legislative body in the world.[7] Wyoming, with less that 500,000 people, and California with roughly 35 million people are both accorded two members in the U.S. Senate. In the *Reynolds* decision the Court made many important proclamations with respect to representation and redistricting. The Equal Protection Clause requires reasonably equal representation in state governments regardless of where someone lives in a state—related to this point is that weighted voting based on geography is discriminatory. Every single person should have one vote and nobody's vote should count more than anyone else's. Both houses of state legislatures need to be based primarily on population, although there is more wiggle room for deviations from ideal population in each district for state legislative lines than for congressional district lines. This is to allow for the smaller state legislative districts to better preserve communities of interest and political subdivisions. Just because the federal government has a chamber in the legislature based on geography and not population, does not imply that states can mimic this kind of representation system.

Nearly simultaneously to the *Reynolds* decision was another landmark case that declared districts for the federal U.S. House of Representatives must be equally populated within each state. In *Wesberry v. Sanders* (1964) the Court ruled on a case that originated in the state of Georgia. At the time the lawsuit was filed the fifth congressional district in Georgia was two to three times larger than some of the other districts in the state. This meant that the voters in this district had substantially less say in federal policies than fellow Georgians who just happened to live somewhere else in the state. The Court ruled that this kind of discrepancy is unconstitutional and the state needs to draw election district lines for the House in a way that districts within the state are substantially equal in population.

Since these landmark decisions, every redistricting plan has had to deal with creating districts that are nearly or exactly equal in population. It is easy to compute what the ideal population for districts within a state should be: simply divided the total population of the state by the number of districts that need to be drawn. So if a state has 4.8 million residents and the state receives eight congressional districts, the ideal population of a district is 600,000 people. For seats in the House of Representatives the amount of leeway that a state has in deviating from this ideal are truly minimal. For instance in 2002 a federal three-judge panel initially struck down a Pennsylvania map for a deviation of 19 people! The largest district in the state had 646,380 people according to the 2000 census and the smallest district had 646,361 people. The difference is, of course, trivial—19 people amounts to less than .003 percent of the total district population. The Republicans, who drew the map, could have convinced the Court that this trivial difference ought to be overlooked, but the problem was that they had no justification whatsoever for why they did not "zero out" the population differences between the districts. The technician who was drawing the maps testified that his boss told him that they had done enough to get the districts to the 19 person deviation. Since deviations from ideal do have to be justified on some grounds, the judges decided to strike the plan down since they thought (correctly) that a plan with no population deviations was possible to draw and there was no apparent reason for the 19 person deviation in the map that was put into place by the Pennsylvania state government. The same three-judge panel reversed themselves two weeks later by allowing the map to stay in place for the 2002 election and the Republicans, who controlled the state government in Pennsylvania, tweaked the map slightly to eliminate the deviations.[8]

Deviations from ideal population are frowned upon by judges much more heavily for congressional districts than for state legislative districts. Congressional district deviations must be justified on the basis of a rational state policy or be found to be unavoidable despite a good faith effort to draw districts with equal population (*Karcher v. Daggett* (1983)). As a result, House districts are almost always equally populous within a state. Table 4.1 shows the deviations from ideal population for all 50 states for congressional districts and both chambers of the state legislatures. Most states have virtually no deviation (i.e., a range of zero, one, or two people), although there are significant exceptions to this rule. Of the 43 states that have multiple congressional districts, 21 of these states have a deviation range of two people or fewer. The largest deviation range is in the state of Idaho where the difference between the smallest district and largest district is 3,595 people. Only five states have a percent overall range of greater than 0.10 percent and none of the states deviate by more than 0.60 percent from ideal. Iowa is one state that had a significant deviation (134 people) in their map enacted after the 2000 census, but there was a worthy justification behind this deviation—the map kept every single county in Iowa whole. This means that no county was split between districts— a feat that is virtually impossible to do with small population deviations. Iowa was just plain lucky to be able to draw districts with such a small deviation in population that were also composed entirely of whole counties.

Insisting that states draw districts with no population deviation is rather extreme, particularly when one considers that the data being used are already over a year old and the data were never correct in the first place. While the Census Bureau does a remarkably good job of counting each person in the country every decade, this task is not done without making millions of errors.[9] So why adhere to strict population equality when the data are relatively old and only estimates of the true population? One really good reason for this strictness is that zero is the only deviation that is not arbitrary. Any other standard, be it a percentage (e.g., .50 percent deviation), or a number (e.g., districts can deviate by 750 people) is completely arbitrary.

For state legislative districts the amount of leeway to draw districts that deviate from the ideal population is much higher. Indeed, deviations of up to 10 percent are quite common. However, the 10 percent figure is not what lawyers call a "safe harbor," which means that the deviations should still have

*Table 4.1* State population deviations for congressional and state legislative districts

| State | 2000 Congressional Plan | | | 2000 State House Plan | | 2000 State Senate Plan | |
|---|---|---|---|---|---|---|---|
| | Ideal district size | Percent overall range | Overall range (no. of people) | Ideal district size | Percent overall range | Ideal district size | Percent overall range |
| Alabama | 635,300 | 0.00% | 0 | 42,353 | 9.93% | 127,060 | 9.73% |
| Alaska | N/A | N/A | N/A | 15,673 | 9.96% | 31,346 | 9.32% |
| Arizona | 641,329 | 0.00% | 0 | 171,021 | 3.79% | 171,021 | 3.79% |
| Arkansas | 668,350 | 0.04% | 303 | 26,734 | 9.87% | 76,383 | 9.81% |
| California | 639,088 | 0.00% | 1 | 423,395 | 0.00% | 846,791 | 0.00% |
| Colorado | 614,465 | 0.00% | 2 | 66,173 | 4.88% | 122,863 | 4.95% |
| Connecticut | 681,113 | 0.00% | 0 | 22,553 | 9.20% | 94,599 | 8.03% |
| Delaware | N/A | N/A | N/A | 19,112 | 9.98% | 37,314 | 9.96% |
| Florida | 639,295 | 0.00% | 1 | 133,186 | 2.79% | 399,559 | 0.03% |
| Georgia | 629,727 | 0.01% | 72 | 45,480 | 1.96% | 146,187 | 1.94% |
| Hawaii | 605,769 | 0.32% | 1,899 | 22,833 | 20.10% | 46,579 | 38.90% |
| Idaho | 646,977 | 0.60% | 3,595 | 36,970 | 9.70% | 36,970 | 9.70% |
| Illinois | 653,647 | 0.00% | 0 | 105,248 | 0.00% | 210,496 | 0.00% |
| Indiana | 675,609 | 0.02% | 102 | 60,805 | 1.92% | 121,610 | 3.80% |
| Iowa | 585,265 | 0.02% | 134 | 29,263 | 1.89% | 58,526 | 1.46% |
| Kansas | 672,105 | 0.00% | 33 | 21,378 | 9.95% | 66,806 | 9.27% |
| Kentucky | 673,628 | 0.00% | 2 | 40,418 | 10.00% | 106,362 | 9.53% |
| Louisiana | 638,425 | 0.04% | 240 | 42,561 | 9.88% | 114,589 | 9.95% |
| Maine | 637,462 | 0.00% | 23 | 8,443 | 9.33% | 36,426 | 3.57% |
| Maryland | 662,061 | 0.00% | 2 | 37,564 | 9.89% | 112,691 | 9.91% |
| Massachusetts | 634,910 | 0.39% | 2476 | 39,682 | 9.68% | 158,727 | 9.33% |
| Michigan | 662,563 | 0.00% | 1 | 90,350 | 9.92% | 261,538 | 9.92% |
| Minnesota | 614,935 | 0.00% | 1 | 36,713 | 1.56% | 73,425 | 1.35% |
| Mississippi | 711,165 | 0.00% | 10 | 23,317 | 9.98% | 54,705 | 9.30% |
| Missouri | 621,690 | 0.00% | 1 | 34,326 | 6.08% | 164,565 | 6.81% |
| Montana | N/A | N/A | N/A | 9,022 | 9.85% | 18,044 | 9.82% |
| Nebraska | 570,421 | 0.00% | 0 | N/A | N/A | 34,924 | 9.21% |
| Nevada | 666,086 | 0.00% | 6 | 47,578 | 1.97% | 95,155 | 9.91% |
| New Hampshire | 617,893 | 0.10% | 636 | 3,089 | 9.26% | 51,491 | 9.50% |
| New Jersey | 647,257 | 0.00% | 1 | 210,359 | 1.83% | 210,359 | 1.83% |
| New Mexico | 606,349 | 0.03% | 166 | 25,986 | 9.70% | 43,311 | 9.60% |
| New York | 654,360 | 0.00% | 1 | 126,510 | 9.43% | 306,072 | 9.78% |
| North Carolina | 619,178 | 0.00% | 1 | 67,078 | 9.98% | 160,986 | 9.96% |
| North Dakota | N/A | N/A | N/A | 13,664 | 10.00% | 13,664 | 10.00% |
| Ohio | 630,730 | 0.00% | 0 | 114,678 | 12.46% | 344,035 | 8.81% |
| Oklahoma | 690,131 | 0.00% | 1 | 34,165 | 2.05% | 71,889 | 4.71% |
| Oregon | 684,280 | 0.00% | 1 | 57,023 | 1.90% | 114,047 | 1.77% |
| Pennsylvania | 646,371 | 0.00% | 1 | 60,498 | 5.54% | 245,621 | 3.98% |
| Rhode Island | 524,160 | 0.00% | 6 | 13,978 | 9.88% | 27,587 | 9.91% |
| South Carolina | 668,669 | 0.00% | 2 | 32,355 | 4.99% | 87,218 | 9.87% |
| South Dakota | N/A | N/A | N/A | 21,567 | 9.69% | 21,567 | 9.69% |
| Tennessee | 632,143 | 0.00% | 5 | 57,467 | 9.99% | 172,402 | 9.98% |
| Texas | 651,619 | 0.00% | 1 | 139,012 | 9.74% | 672,639 | 9.71% |
| Utah | 744,390 | 0.00% | 1 | 29,776 | 8.00% | 77,006 | 7.02% |
| Vermont | N/A | N/A | N/A | 4,059 | 18.99% | 20,234 | 14.28% |
| Virginia | 643,501 | 0.00% | 38 | 70,785 | 3.90% | 176,963 | 4.00% |

| State | 2000 Congressional Plan | | | 2000 State House Plan | | 2000 State Senate Plan | |
| | Ideal district size | Percent overall range | Overall range (no. of people) | Ideal district size | Percent overall range | Ideal district size | Percent overall range |
|---|---|---|---|---|---|---|---|
| Washington | 654,902 | 0.00% | 7 | 120,288 | 0.30% | 120,288 | 0.30% |
| West Virginia | 602,781 | 0.22% | 1,313 | 18,083 | 9.98% | 106,374 | 10.92% |
| Wisconsin | 670,459 | 0.00% | 5 | 54,179 | 1.60% | 162,536 | 0.98% |
| Wyoming | N/A | N/A | N/A | 8,230 | 9.81% | 16,459 | 9.51% |

* Data are from Census Bureau data and NCSL www.ncsl.org/programs/legman/redistrict/redistpopdev.htm

some guiding principle behind them. What kinds of justifications are usually accepted by a court? Justifications usually involve preserving communities of interest—not dividing cities, counties, or other political subdivisions among districts; avoiding pairing incumbents; preservation of the cores of previous districts.

While there are some very reasonable justifications for allowing population deviations among districts within a state, the benefits do not outweigh the likely costs in my mind. Arguments in favor of deviations usually revolve around issues such as compactness and communities of interest. If we relax the one person one vote rule, then we could keep more municipalities and counties whole; we could draw more compact districts insofar as we would not have to extend many districts into more populated areas to ease the problem of populating each district equally; we might avoid some redistricting related lawsuits because as soon as the new census data are released every electoral map across the country is instantly unconstitutional because of population changes over the course of the last decade. Reducing the role of courts in the redistricting process makes legislatures more important in this inherently political process, which is beneficial to both the courts and the people.[10] While I am sympathetic to many of these arguments, the fact of the matter is that allowing deviations is an invitation to gerrymander—the allure of gerrymandering is enticing enough to politicians without us sending out embossed invitations with lacy bows on fine linen paper. When we do invite this kind of behavior, we cannot be surprised when we get it.

For example, in the Alaska state legislative redistricting after the 2000 census, the Alaska Redistricting Board was controlled by a majority of people sympathetic to the Democrats. Not surprisingly, the board approved a redistricting map that favored the Democrat candidates (just as the Republicans would have done if they were in control). One of the many tools that the Board used to gerrymander the map was to utilize population deviations to their advantage. If you want to elect more Democrats, you simply underpopulate Democratic-leaning districts, and over-populate Republican-leaning districts. This allows the Democrats to win more seats per vote than the Republicans. In this case 13 of the 40 House seats in the state legislature leaned Democratic. Ten of these districts had population totals less than ideal (i.e., they were under-populated). Of the 25 seats than leaned toward the Republicans, 16 of these districts had population total above the ideal population. On average Democratic districts were more than 2 percent under the ideal, while Republican districts were nearly 1.5 percent above the ideal. This pattern was duplicated for the Alaskan state senate as well. This plan was thrown out by the Alaskan state Supreme Court, in part because of these deviations, and an amended map was eventually put into place that was fair to both political parties. The board was split three–two in favor of the first plan and the amended plan devised after the state Supreme Court ruling was passed unanimously by all five members of the board.

Another recent example of this comes from the state legislative districting in Georgia. Governor Roy Barnes (D) and his Democratic colleagues in the state legislature drew a map that "packed as many voters as possible into districts in Republican-leaning areas, while spreading out traditional Democratic voters in as many districts as possible. That effectively makes a voter's ballot in one of the packed districts worth less than a vote in an underpopulated district. The maps disregarded 'traditional redistricting criteria' such as compactness, protecting communities of interest, and keeping counties intact. The judges said map-drawers would have had more leeway with population differences if they were trying to achieve these goals."[11]

Thus requiring a strict adherence to making all district equally populous, even though we are talking about using census data that are over a year old and not perfectly accurate to begin with, makes a great deal of sense when one considers the chicanery possible when the door is left open for drawing unequal districts.

## Contiguity

Contiguity is a strict requirement in congressional and state legislative districting. A district cannot have multiple discrete sections, which is to say every point in a district must be reachable from any other point in the same district without leaving the district. The only exceptions to this rule are for islands, in which case the Court recognizes water contiguity. This principle is relatively noncontroversial, since without it the idea of single-member districts makes much less sense.

It would be much easier to draw a fair partisan plan with noncontiguous districts, but at that point it would be much easier to institute a statewide proportional representation plan. A noncontiguous districting plan would simply be composed of differing size pockets of the population that need not be connected together. It might look like a modern work of art with various size freckles, some red and some blue, covering the entire state. Figure 4.1 shows a noncontiguous district, on the left, and then a contiguous one on the

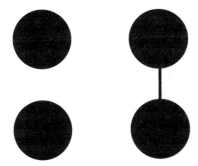

*Figure 4.1* Contiguity.

right. Connecting the two separate pockets of population by a thin strip of land is a perfectly acceptable approach to preserving contiguity. Often electoral districts will be made up of small thin "fingers" or "necks" that connect one part of the district to another. Some times these strips of land will run along the freeway or other unpopulated parts of the state.

While dropping the contiguity requirement would surely make the job of drawing districts that treat the parties fairly much easier, it fundamentally changes the nature of the single-member district system and would surely be ruled illegal or unconstitutional. A packed plan with entirely contiguous districts is certainly possible in every state, but not without a cost, as the districts might take on rather odd shapes. Which brings us to the next principle— compact districts.

## Compactness

The term "gerrymander" stemmed from a rather peculiar-looking district drawn by Massachusetts Governor Gerry in 1811 and since that time there has been considerable attention paid to the shape of congressional and legislative districts. Compactness is a matter of geometry, and while geographers and social scientists have come up with literally dozens of ways to try to measure compactness no one has agreed on a single measure. Indeed, at some level, compactness refers to the degree to which districts are "pleasing to the eye." Hebert et al. (1997) summarize it nicely when they write: "The smoother a district's border, and the more its shape resembles a square or a circle rather than a spider or a string bean, the more likely it will be deemed 'compact'."[12] So compactness has nothing to do with the size of a district—the area of a district is immaterial inasmuch as each district needs to contain the same number of people not the same number of square miles.

Compactness is one of the redistricting principles that is less well followed than some of the other principles, such as contiguousness and equal population. Probably the most important consideration about compactness that makes this so is that there is no best way to measure it. Indeed, various scholars have shown that any single measure devised thus far cannot detect different kinds of deviations from compact shapes.[13] Some metrics use the ratio of the length of a district to the width of the district, others use variations of methods that use the area of the district compared to the perimeter of the district. One of the more commonly used methods was proposed by Ernest Reock.[14] He argued that circles are the "most compact plane, for here the maximum area is enclosed within a given perimeter"[15] and therefore circles are the ideal shape for compact districts. So Reock concluded that a good measurement of a district's compactness is to take a district and circumscribe it with the smallest circle possible then compare the area of the district to the area of the circumscribing circle. The closer this ratio is to one, the more compact the district. While the logic behind Reock's metric is solid, there are problems with his proposal. Ideal districts are circular but it is not possible to divide a polygon into a group of circles. More importantly though is the fact that his method does not punish very jagged edges in a district, as long as the district is relatively circular it would be scored as compact. Thus Figure 4.2 shows a compact districts in the shape of a circle and a square. However, Figure 4.3 is circular but with very jagged edges, so it would do well on some measures of compactness but not others. Figure 4.4 is an example of a district that would not, and should not score well on virtually any measure of compactness.

Young surveys various measures and finds that "some of these measures are better than others, all are defective in some crucial respect; that is, they fail to give satisfactory results on certain types of geographical configurations. The

*Figure 4.2*

*Figure 4.3*

Figure 4.4

conclusion is that 'compactness' is not a sufficiently precise concept to be used as legal standard for districting plans."[16] Perhaps the best, and certainly the simplest approach is to visually inspect the maps and look at the shapes of the various districts. It is not too hard to spot ugly districts. It takes just a glance at the congressional district map for Georgia that was in effect for 2002–04 to see that there are some really odd-shaped districts. Figures 4.5 and 4.6 are maps of the congressional districts of Georgia during this time period. Figure 4.5 represents the whole state, while Figure 4.6 is a more detailed map of the Atlanta area districts. Looking at the entire state there are some particularly odd parts for several districts, such as how district 1 snakes up well into the central part of district 3, and district 12 snakes up through the middle of district 9. Moreover, the sheer ugliness of several districts is quite apparent in Figure 4.6 especially districts 8, 11, and 13. Districts 7 and 9 are also oddly configured. Compare these districts to the revised districts that took effect for the 2006 elections in Figures 4.7 and 4.8. Just glancing at the revised figures one gets an immediate sense that the compactness of districts is much better. We do not need any quantifiable metrics to conclude that the revised map is significantly more compact that the previous one.

Decisions from the Supreme Court have made it clear that that shape of districts do in fact matter. For instance, in the *Shaw v. Reno* decision the Court proclaimed that "reapportionment is one area in which appearances do matter." The infamous twelfth district in North Carolina, which spawned a series of Supreme Court decisions, was struck down in part because of its odd shape. In effect, the Court ruled, the map makers had ignored other traditional districting principles and concentrated almost exclusively on race. In a related case *Miller v. Johnson* (1995) the Court was specific about criteria that they thought important to draw districts:

> The plaintiff's burden is to show, either through circumstantial evidence of a district's shape and demographics or more direct evidence going to

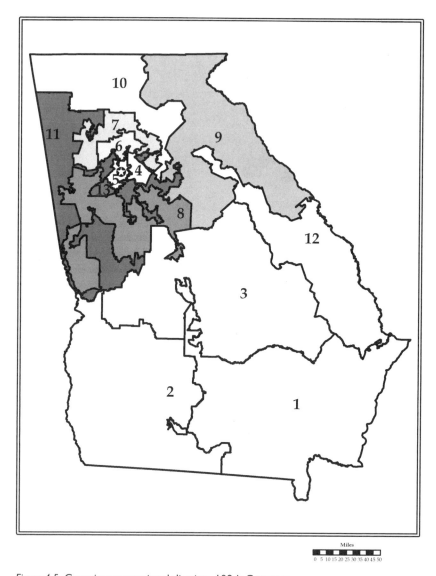

*Figure 4.5* Georgia: congressional districts, 108th Congress.

*Note:* Numbers indicate congressional districts.
*Source:* Clark Bensen, Polidata.org. Used with permission.

legislative purpose, that race was the predominant factor motivating the legislature's decision to place a significant number of voters within or without a particular district. To make this showing, a plaintiff must prove that the legislature subordinated traditional race-neutral districting prin-

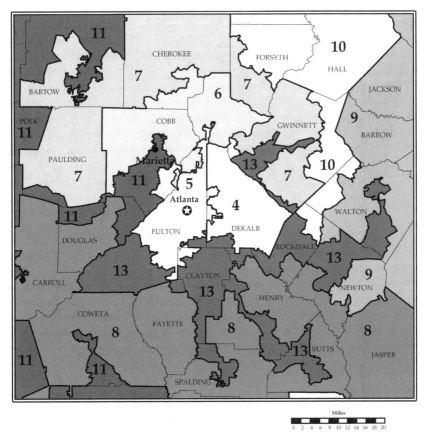

*Figure 4.6* Georgia, Greater Atlanta: congressional districts, 108th Congress.

*Note:* Numbers indicate congressional districts.
*Source:* Clark Bensen, Polidata.org. Used with permission.

ciples, including but not limited to compactness, contiguity, respect for political subdivisions or communities defined by actual shared interest, to racial considerations.

An added complication is that sometimes the natural boundaries that are often used in redistricting, such as county or municipal boundaries, rivers, etc., might not lend themselves to compact districts. A river or city boundary might be nonlinear (i.e., ugly) to begin with, so the district might appear to make no sense geographically, when in fact it does. Nonetheless, compactness, like many districting principles, is important but not necessarily strictly required in a map.

The Supreme Court has not put its imprimatur on any measure of compactness and thus redistricters have no clear guidance on what shapes are allowed

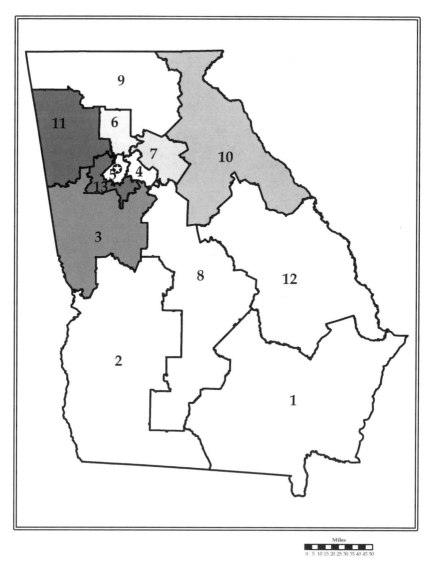

*Figure 4.7* Georgia: congressional districts, 110th Congress.

*Note:* Numbers indicate congressional districts.
*Source:* Clark Bensen, Polidata.org. Used with permission.

and which will be thrown out. Thus, there is a great deal of latitude as to just how ugly districts can be before a judge will object (such as those in the 2002 Georgia map for instance). Deviations from ideal can be successfully defended as long as there is some underlying principle that explains why a map did not satisfy the equal population requirement, or why districts are not particularly

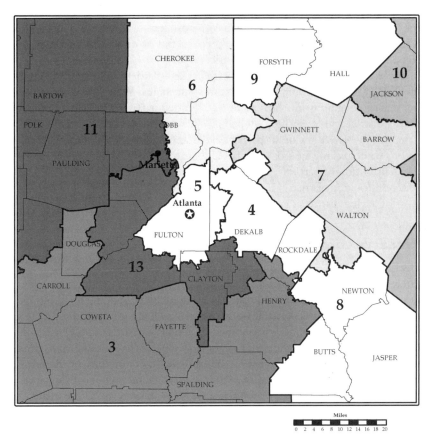

*Figure 4.8* Georgia, Greater Atlanta: congressional districts, 110th Congress.

*Note:* Numbers indicate congressional districts.
*Source:* Clark Bensen, Polidata.org. Used with permission.

compact. For instance, one could argue that while some of the individual districts may be poorly shaped, the other criteria for redistricting were maximized (i.e., protect incumbents, preserve political subdivisions, etc.). If a districting plan goes to great lengths (i.e., draws districts with tortured shapes) to satisfy partisan fairness, then I suspect it would be unlikely that a judge would force the state to draw a new map on the basis of compactness alone.

It is not clear to me that compactness is particularly important in drawing electoral boundaries. There is nothing inherently good (evil) about particularly eye-pleasing (ugly) districts. It is possible to draw an incredibly unfair and gerrymandered map using very compact, well-shaped districts. Similarly, ugly districts may in fact be satisfying another more important principle in a plan, such as drawing a majority–minority district. In general, very odd-shaped districts may be suggestive that something is afoot, but this is not necessarily the case. Nor should we assume a map with nothing but squares and rectangles is impartial in its treatment of the political parties or minorities. These issues run parallel to the compactness of districts.

Implementing a fair partisan plan with packed districts will almost certainly involve drawing noncompact districts in some states. While there are always pockets of geography in which many like-minded partisans reside, in order to draw a district with over 600,000 people likely to support a Republican candidate, this involves drawing districts to avoid any significant Democratic population, while picking up pockets of Republicans. This process, depending on the distribution of partisans in a state, could easily force map makers to draw very odd-looking districts. However, the benefits of a fair plan far outweigh the costs of having districts that look like bug splats on a windshield.

## Preserve communities of interest

Districts are supposed to be drawn so that they encompass a community of interest. This is to say district lines are artificial, but they should not be drawn in such a way that the resultant constellation of districts is completely arbitrary, but rather they should contain, as the Supreme Court put it in the *Miller v. Johnson* decision, "communities defined by actual shared interests." This concept can be particularly slippery since any competent lawyer can spin a tale about how any district represents some underlying community of interest.[17] However, the Supreme Court has tried to give some teeth to what they mean by this term. In the *Miller v. Johnson* case the Court rejected the eleventh district in Georgia, which was a majority black district but it combined poor black neighborhoods from Chatham county with black neighborhoods in Atlanta. These regions according to the Court were "260 miles apart in distance and worlds apart in culture."

Given the contiguity and compactness principles outlined above, it is not particularly surprising that communities of interest tend to be geographically based. Preserving like-minded communities often boils down to keeping as many counties and municipalities whole within separate districts. For example, it has become commonplace for districting plans to summarize the number of city and county "splits" that they contain. This is clearly not a perfect measure of how well a map preserves communities of interest but it is a way to quantify the concept. Looking at virtually any congressional district map makes it quite clear that country boundaries really do serve as the fundamental building block for most congressional districts. Of course, Texas was the most notorious state in the last few years with respect to redistricting because of the so-called re-redistricting that took place in the state engineered by former Republican representative Tom Delay. Figure 4.9 is a map of the congressional districts in Texas as of 2006. Texas is a good state to use as an example because it is large and has many small counties. The smaller sub-units on the map are

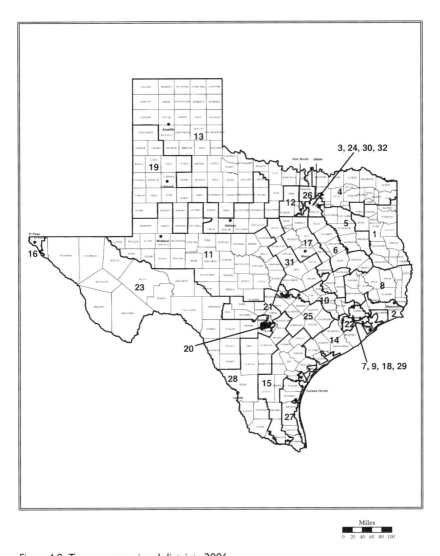

*Figure 4.9* Texas congressional districts 2006.

Note: Numbers indicate congressional districts.
Source: Clark Bensen, Polidata.org. Used with permission.

the 254 counties in Texas and the larger regions are the various congressional districts. The counties are the primary building block for congressional districts and it is easy to see how congressional district lines for those districts that encompass larger, less populated regions of the state, follow along county lines.

As Butler and Cain point out, many of the principles guiding districting are in tension with one another.[18] So, for instance, if we require that districts are equally populous, then this means that counties and cities will certainly need to be split. Thus, we have to balance our desire to maximize one principle (one person one vote) against the desire to maximize another (keeping counties whole to the extent possible). While the extent to which a district keeps a community of interest together is something that gets brought up in litigation where the discussion can center around how certain parts of the district have shared interests and shared goals, in my mind preserving communities of interest has devolved into a contest to see which districting map can split the fewest counties and cities.

I argue that communities of interest, properly defined, should be conceived around shared ideology, and not be based on geography. For instance, is Albany, New York a community of interest? What about Coconino County Arizona? The only time they really constitute a set of people with coherent unified interests is when we are talking about parochial governmental projects. So if we are talking about the federal government setting aside money for a new bridge across the Fox River in Illinois, almost all of the local citizens are likely to support the idea. However, if the issue is anything substantive— should we privatize social security or should we increase taxes or should we end the war in Iraq—then there will naturally be a division among the citizens in nearly any geographic region. Geographic constituencies are limited in truly being a communities of interest by the nature of the distribution of ideological preferences within the locality.

The liberal-leaning citizens of upstate New York or northern Arizona do constitute a community of interest. They are going to agree on the important issues that face our country in addition to issues that only affect their community. The single dimension left–right (liberal–conservative) continuum is what defines politics in America, so draw districts to keep all people that live in roughly the same part of a state who think about politics in a similar fashion together, not to keep everyone that happens to live in the same city or a county in a single district. I do favor relaxing the compactness requirement to the extent necessary so that we can draw districts packed with like-minded Americans. If we can draw homogeneous districts that are also compact and preserve county lines, all the better, but we should not be overly focused on drawing "pretty" districts or keeping counties whole when these districts contain sharp divisions among the beliefs about substantive politics in the country.

## Protecting incumbents

Incumbent members of Congress are keenly interested in redistricting for obvious reasons. Since redistricting is done by each state government, this is one instance in which members of Congress are reliant upon state legislators for their political future. It strikes many people as odd that protecting current incumbents is a reasonable goal for map makers. The Supreme Court has recognized this goal in their decision in the *Bush v. Vera* case. Justice O'Connor writes for the Court in the majority opinion: "We have recognized incumbency protection, at least in the limited form of avoiding contests between incumbent(s), as a legitimate state goal" (116 S. Ct. 1954). Pairing incumbents is one of the standard methods for one party to remove incumbents from the other party. For instance, the Texas Republicans targeted, among other Democrats, Representative Martin Frost as one person they would like to see lose his seat. To do this they redrew Frost's district so that he was paired against Republican Representative Pete Sessions in a district that leaned Republican. While this strategy does not always work, in this case it did when Sessions beat Frost in a hotly contested election in 2004. Sometimes this strategy is called "kidnapping."

A district is defined as "belonging" to one incumbent or another on the basis of where the incumbent's main residence is. While the Constitution only requires that a representative live in the state from which she is elected and not the specific district she represents (indeed there is no Constitutional requirement that we have single member districts as all), it would be difficult, if not impossible, for someone to be elected in a district other than the one in which she resides.

An example of the difficulty in applying this strategy comes to us from the 2002 Pennsylvania redistricting process. The Republicans controlled the districting process in that state and, without surprise, drew a map that favored the Republican Party. One Democrat they targeted was Representative Frank Mascara. Mascara had represented the twentieth district of Pennsylvania for four terms when the map was redrawn. Most of Mascara's old district was put into the new twelfth congressional district, while Mascara's house was put into a newly constituted eighteenth district that leaned Republican, and Mascara concluded that he probably could not win there. He decided to run in the twelfth district, which also included the residence of incumbent Democratic member John Murtha. This meant that Mascara had to take on a fellow incumbent Democrat in the primary with the distinct disadvantage of not living in the district. The primary was hard fought, and at times quite nasty, but Murtha prevailed in a landslide (64 percent to 36 percent).

There are many very good reasons for protecting incumbents in the redistricting process. First, the incumbents have been previously elected by the people, so removing them by jiggling the lines is, in a sense, undemocratic. Next, they have seniority in the House of Representatives and the more senior members typically have more power and influence than those with less seniority. This can translate directly into federal dollars for the district and the state since committee chairmen are drawn from the ranks of more senior members and they have the ability to extract more money for projects in their district. Clearly there are instances in which pairing sitting incumbents is impossible to avoid—if a state loses one or more seats after the census and no one voluntarily retires, then there will have to be an election with two incumbents vying for the same seat. The packed partisan plan I suggest in this book would make it no more or less difficult to protect incumbents when drawing new electoral boundaries.

## The Voting Rights Act and related racial issues

Race plays a central and important role in the modern redistricting process. Crafty line drawing was one of the many ways in which racial minorities were kept out of the political process. For instance, if there is a large number of African Americans living in the inner city, but those in power want to minimize the extent to which these citizens are capable of electing someone to represent their interests, all one has to do is to crack this population across several districts so that African Americans make up a numerical minority in each district. Another method used to dilute the power of racial minorities in America was not to draw any districts at all. Instead, a state would just elect representatives in a single "at-large" district. So if the state consisted of 30 percent black people and there are five districts, there may very well have to be at least one black majority district, but if everyone gets five votes to elect five people, and the majority group, in this example white people, vote with a high degree of cohesion, then the minority group will always lose (this is true for any numerical minority, not just racial minorities).

The Voting Rights Act, originally passed in 1965, has had a major impact on redistricting and the role that race plays in this process. The two relevant sections of the Voting Rights Act are Sections 2 and 5. Section 2 applies to the entire country, while Section 5 applies to nine whole states (Alabama, Alaska, Arizona, Georgia, Louisiana, Mississippi, South Carolina, Texas, and Virginia) and parts of seven others (California, Florida, Michigan, New Hampshire, New York, North Carolina, and South Dakota).

Section 5 of the Voting Rights Act covers only part of the country, so 34 states do not have to concern themselves with this part of the law. For the other 16, Section 5 plays an important part in any changes the state wants to make to its laws regarding elections. This part of the law was included because some states, primarily in the South, would come up with new laws to discriminate against minority voters as quickly as the federal courts would strike down old laws. In a nutshell, for any jurisdiction covered under this section, *any* change in election law must be precleared with the federal government. The state must show the federal government that the proposed change in election law would not discriminate in both purpose and effect. So it cannot be purposefully or accidentally discriminatory against minorities. Obviously a new redistricting map is going to constitute a major change in election law and would therefore have to be precleared, but this process, as I mentioned previously, covers any change. So if a water district wants to change the location of a polling place for an upcoming election, it must get this precleared by the feds before it can take place. Preclearance can happen one of two ways—

through the Department of Justice or the United States District Court for the District of Columbia.

The effects prong of Section 5 means that the change in the law should not lead to "retrogression" of the position of the racial or language minority group. How can one tell if the new law has a retrogressive effect? By comparing it to the benchmark plan, which is the current constellation of districts that is in effect. In states with majority–minority districts, retrogression often boils down to the number of majority–minority districts and the proportion of minorities in the state itself. So if a state has two majority Hispanic districts currently, this is the benchmark. If a new map draws just a single majority–minority district, the map is likely to be denied preclearance. So this part of the law simply forces some states to get permission from the federal government before they change any of their election laws.

Section 2 really reinforces what was intended with the Fifteenth Amendment to the Constitution. The law expressly prohibits any election procedures that "results in a denial or abridgement of the right of any citizen . . . to vote on account of race or color." The law is also specific insofar as it supplies a "test" as to when we know if someone's rights have been abridged—if the process is not equally open to minorities or if they have less opportunity than other people to participate in the process or elect representatives of their choice.

In 1986 the Supreme Court decided *Thornburg v. Gingles* in which the Court gave some specificity to Section 2 in terms of the redistricting process. In this case the Court laid out certain conditions that, if met, forced a state to draw districts specifically so that minority voters would "have a reasonable opportunity to elect a candidate of their choice." The three conditions can be summed up as follows:

1    The minority group in question has to be significantly large and compact enough to constitute a majority in a single-member district.
2    The minority group needs to be "politically cohesive," which means they have to vote alike to some degree.
3    The white majority tends to vote in a bloc (i.e., together) in sufficient numbers to typically defeat the candidate that the minority group prefers.

If all of these conditions are met and, given the "totality of the circumstances," the minorities have less opportunity to participate and elect candidates that they prefer, then the state is obligated to draw a "majority–minority" district in which the minority voters are likely to control the outcome.[19] The conditions are relatively straightforward. The question is when should a state be obliged to draw a district in which a candidate that the minority group prefers has a reasonable opportunity to be elected? Well, first there must be a sufficient number of this group in the state to make up a majority of a district and these people cannot be spread randomly throughout the state. Second, the group must be somewhat cohesive politically. If half the group prefers a Democrat and the other half prefers a Republican, then drawing a special district for this set of people makes less sense. Finally, there must be racially polarized voting present in which the white voters tend to vote against the preferred candidate of the black voters.

If the first three prongs are satisfied, there is still a chance that a state may not need to create a majority–minority district and basically it boils down to whether the minority voters in the state are already controlling seats in the legislature in proportion to their overall proportion of the population in a state. So if Hispanics make up 25 percent of the population in the state and 30 percent of the seats state legislature is controlled by Hispanics, then a court is not likely to order an additional majority–minority district to be drawn. The important case for this subsection of redistricting law is a 1994 Supreme Court decision, *Johnson v. De Grandy*. Here the Court decided that a state is not obligated to draw the maximum number of majority–minority districts possible, especially if that would exceed the proportionality test.

The *Gingles* decision in 1986 radically affected what districts looked like in the 1990 round of redistricting. More importantly, it also had a major effect on the number of racial minorities that were able to get elected to the House of Representatives. In 1986, during the 99th Congress there were only 21 African–American members. After the 1990 round of redistricting, which took effect for the 103rd Congress, there were 39 African–American members.[20] There were ten new Hispanic members of Congress elected in the 1992 election alone.[21] As minority populations continue to grow and change, so do the prevalence of these districts. For instance, the Hispanic population continues to grow and so do the number of majority–minority districts. The percentage of African Americans in the country does not change all that much and so the proportion of seats held by African Americans might remain stagnant. Most members of Congress who are African American or Hispanic do come from majority–minority districts.[22]

Scholars and political observers have debated the various effects of these districts since their advent. One example of this debate revolves around the question of whether these districts helped or hurt the Democratic Party. Naturally, these districts heavily favor Democratic candidates since black people and Hispanics tend to be overwhelmingly aligned with the Democratic Party, so the first order effect of adding these kinds of districts is to increase the number of Democrats elected to Congress. However, since these districts were drawn almost exclusively in inner cities throughout the country, the districts were relatively easy to draw with overwhelming majorities of racial minorities. This effectively packed minorities into a few inner-city districts, which had the effect of "bleaching" surrounding congressional districts, increasing the likelihood that Republicans would get elected from these nearby suburban districts.[23] Moreover, majority–minority districts tend to elect very liberal minority Democrats to the House, which could have reinforced the idea among voters that the Democratic Party is the party of racial minorities. This conception could conceivably push moderate white voters away from the Democratic Party toward the Republicans. But there are plenty of others who argue that while this new form of redistricting had some minor impact on the overall partisanship in the House, the aftermath of the *Gingles* decision could be neither credited nor blamed for the reduction in the number of Democratically controlled seats in the House of Representatives in the early 1990s.[24]

Since the *Gingles* decision there have been several important decisions from the Supreme Court (*Shaw v. Reno, Miller v. Johnson,* and *Bush v. Vera*) that have altered racial redistricting to some extent. Through a series of decisions in the 1990s the Court made it clear that race should not be the predominant factor in redistricting. It has to be *a factor*, just not *the factor*. In 1993, in *Shaw v. Reno* the Court struck down an odd-looking district in North Carolina that was drawn to be a second majority black district in the state. The district was drawn because North Carolina is one of the covered jurisdictions under Section 5 of the Voting Rights Act, and after the state submitted a new electoral map for review by the Department of Justice, the state was told to draw a second majority black district. So in order to comply with this decision, a second, rather ugly district was drawn so that there were two majority black districts in the state. The Court decided that the state had gone too far, inasmuch as they forgot about all of the other factors that should affect district shape and drew one exclusively on the basis of race. This decision did not mean that states were not required to draw these districts, but that they were not allowed to make maps solely on the basis of race.

It is beyond the scope of this book to work out all of the effects of majority–minority redistricting or to write a legal primer on racial redistricting, rather we are simply interested in whether or not a fair partisan redistricting approach is compatible with current federal law concerning redistricting and traditional redistricting practices. In terms of the racial aspects of redistricting required by law and prior Court decisions, these pose no problems for a fair partisan approach with districts packed with like-minded people. Indeed, one of the major complaints about majority–minority districts over the years is that they have been overly packed with Democrats. Since these districts are almost always in the inner cities with heavily minority populations, it is not hard to draw districts that are overwhelmingly black, and overwhelmingly Democratic. So in that sense, these districts are, in many ways, the districts that should be emulated around the country.

## Conclusion

There are several important aspects of redistricting that cannot be overlooked when redrafting the electoral boundaries of a state. Districts for the House of Representatives have to be equally populous, and if they are not, then the state had better have a good justification for any deviations. Districts also need to be contiguous and each elect just a single member. These requirements are strict. There are aspects of racial redistricting that some states have to comply with under certain conditions, but beyond the usual suspects, traditional districting criteria can often be played fast and loose. For instance, with compactness, there have been dozens and dozens of examples of extremely ugly districts over the years. I argue there is nothing inherently good about a well-shaped district and if we are interested in maximizing some other principle, such as minority representation, or making a map that improves representation and treats both parties fairly, then drawing less compact districts makes a great deal of sense. The purpose of this chapter was to review the principles that guide redistricters and to show that none of these conditions makes it impossible to transition to a fair packed partisan plan at any time. We do not have to amend the Constitution or even change any federal laws; we just have to adjust our approach to redistricting and our attitudes toward electoral competition.

# Chapter 5

# Why competitive elections are bad and noncompetitive elections are good

In the previous chapter the principles guiding districting drawing were reviewed with an emphasis placed on explaining how a packed partisan plan fits within these guidelines. In this chapter the benefits to such an approach are explained in some detail. What are the costs and benefits to drawing competitive districts? Here I lay out the reasons that drawing districts with the specific goal of enhancing representation by drawing homogeneous districts has very real benefits, and how taking the opposite approach of drawing competitive districts is not appropriate and is actually counter productive to democracy for a variety of reasons. As districts become more homogenous (i.e., the likelihood of competition in the general election decreases), the proportion of winning citizens increases. Voters whose preferred candidate wins the election are much more likely to be well represented in Congress and more likely to have positive attitudes toward the government. Moreover, as long as districts are packed symmetrically between the two parties (i.e., one party's districts are not more heavily packed than the other party's districts), the chances of a gerrymander are zero. It is through the lack of symmetry that one party can gain an advantage over the other through the redistricting process. Related to this point is the idea that nonproportional outcomes are very likely if districts are competitive and very unlikely in a system with packed districts.

## Homogenous districts improve attitudes toward Congress and its members

I demonstrated in chapter 3 that people who vote for the winning candidate are significantly more satisfied with their specific member of Congress, with Congress more generally, and feel more political efficacious than losing voters. By drawing districts packed with like-minded citizens we can significantly reduce the proportion of political "losers" in America. Congress does not enjoy particularly high approval ratings from the citizenry and this is one simple way of increasing the number of people that feel good about their representation in the House of Representatives. Some critics might say "Why should we care about the voters' happiness?" My response is that we should substantively care about the attitudes that Americans have toward the government because dissatisfaction and cynicism can lead to less trust in government. The less the people trust their government, the less likely they are to feel efficacious and participate in the political system through traditional avenues such as voting. I am not contending that competitive congressional districts lead to revolt or political violence, but rather that more trust in government would not hurt the system. For instance Anderson et al. find that "more losers are satisfied with the functioning of democracy than are dissatisfied, that an overwhelming majority believes that the most recent election was fair, and more losers say that parties and politicians care what ordinary people think than the opposite. Thus, we uncovered little evidence of widespread distress among losers across a widely divergent set of countries."[1] If an actor repeatedly feels that the voice option is ineffective for instance, exit becomes more likely. Nicholas Miller puts it nicely: "losers (both politicians and their followers) can likewise console themselves with the thought 'wait until next election'."[2] But once again the prospect is comforting to the losers only insofar as there is some reasonable prospect that the next election may produce a different outcome with different winners and losers.

A homogenous districting approach does not mean we completely eliminate losing voters. In a single-member district electoral system it is impossible to draw districts that are composed entirely of one party or the other. For that we would need to switch to a proportional representation type of system. Rather than that, we are trying to minimize the number and proportion of losing voters across the country while maintaining the single-member district system that American voters have grown accustomed to. Still we can create a homogenous Democratic district which has 20–30 percent Republicans living in it and these voters would have virtually no chance of electing a Republican, and this fact could make their dissatisfaction even more severe than if they resided in a district that at least provided an opportunity for them to elect a candidate of their choice. Recall, however, that the margin of victory had no impact on attitudes toward government for losers. So the key factor is simply losing, not whether you lose by a small or large number of votes. Wasted votes—votes for losing candidates that have no impact on who serves in Congress, are inherent to the single-member district system. The packed partisan plan advocated here explicitly tries to minimize the number and proportion of voters who end up losing.[3] More winners mean more satisfaction with the government and better representation.

## Enhancing representation

America has a republican form of government, which means that people are elected to represent voters' wishes in the federal government. Representation, both as a concept and as a reality, is rather tricky. Absent unanimity among a group (of any size), perfect representation is impossible. Disagreement among members of the group to be represented is central to the sticky problem of representation. Members of the modern House of Representatives each represent hundreds of thousands of people (the average district size in 2007 is about 650,000 people). While some of these districts are fairly homogeneous, there is some degree of ideological diversity for every single one of these districts and the more diversity there is among the populous, the more difficult it is for an individual to represent the views of the people. This is analogous to the notion of statistical sampling. Important information and interesting conclusions about a population can de drawn based upon a relatively small sample from the total population, even if we are talking about millions of people. For instance, we can get a rough idea how the country is going to vote in an upcoming presidential election by sampling around 1,000 to 1,500 people (this is the typical sample size of the ubiquitous polls run by the various news organizations). Another way of thinking about this is that a chef can tell if her soup needs more salt by tasting just a spoonful—she need not consume the entire pot. However, in order for this to be true, the soup has to be homogeneous, and, thankfully for all chefs, with a couple stirs with a whisk, it will be. The more heterogeneity that exists in a population, the less well it can be represented by a sample. This is not to say that diverse districts are harder to poll accurately, the point I am trying to make is that the average support for the president in a diverse district might be 50 percent, while in a homogeneous one it might be 90 percent. Votes in the House of Representatives are either "yea" or "nay" and each member must vote one way or another. Unless all the citizens of a district are uniformly in favor or against a bill, each time a representative casts a vote, she is voting the opposite way that some of her constituents want her to vote. If the representative knows her constituency well and is doing a good job, this proportion is less than half of the likely voters in the next election.

Any form of representation is going to suffer some amount of agency loss. Which is to say the person "standing in" for another person or group of persons is incapable of doing *exactly* as the principal wants all the time. Even when a single person is representing one other person, there is bound to be some amount of agency loss. We make the representative's job more difficult by having to represent two or three people. It becomes increasingly complex as the size of the constituency grows. As a general rule, as the size of the constituency grows so does the diversity of opinion in the constituency. Presidential, senatorial, and gubernatorial elections in America are all from fixed constituencies (i.e., the states) and thus there is nothing we can do about diversity of constituencies. However, for state legislative and congressional elections we can draw districts so that diversity within districts is minimized. This might increase diversity across districts in a state, but that is not a problem, in fact the diversity of a state should be reflected across districts in the state (just not within districts).

The major problem with competitive districts is that the closer the general election, the more difficult it is to accurately represent the views of all constituents in a district. Exciting elections boil down to fewer people being represented accurately in Congress. Worse still is that redistricting can effectively disenfranchise millions of voters across the country by putting them in districts where their preferred candidate will almost always certainly lose. One of the downsides to a single-member district electoral system is that inevitably there will be a significant proportion of the voting electorate whose votes are wasted (i.e., they vote for a losing candidate and end up with no representation). Effective gerrymandering can even situate districts in such a way that a party can receive a majority of the votes and end up with less than a majority of the seats.

Competitive districts are also tricky from the point of view of the elected official. Assuming the incumbent cares about getting reelected, and the extant political science literature suggests that incumbents do,[4] he has to figure out how to carve a reelection constituency out of his district. He has to act, vote, and secure federal dollars in such a way as to maximize the likelihood that a majority of the people that show up in the next election will cast a ballot in his favor.[5] In a competitive district roughly half the electorate will favor this candidate and the other half will oppose him. But the electorate is not perfectly black and white as there are moderate voters, who identify with both major parties, who are willing to vote for candidates from the other party. So how does a representative vote in order to successfully be reelected? The answer is not clear. One option is to take a strict party line. So if a Democrat is elected by just couple hundred votes in order to hang on to all of those voters, he will decide to be as liberal as possible to please his Democratic leaning constituents. Naturally, he is not going to be a hero to the 49 percent of his district that is Republican or more conservative.

Fiorina[6] and Huntington[7] both theorize that the members of Congress who are most likely to toe the party line are those that are elected by the narrowest of margins. In order to preserve their relatively small reelection constituency, the marginal members are going to be very liberal if they are Democrats, or very conservative if they are Republicans. Using what he terms as "weak data," Fiorina compares the average change in Conservative coalition support scores for those districts which switch party but are marginal and those districts which switch party but are "safe" (won with 60 percent or more of the vote) for the 88th through 90th Congresses. His findings demonstrate that the difference is greater in the marginal switch districts. Members from marginal districts are thus, not policy moderates. Huntington provides data which show that the policy spread between members of Congress in marginal districts is greater than that between members from safe districts. Because of the close link between ideology and party loyalty, the implication of these results is that members from marginal districts are also likely to be more loyal to their party.

A second option is for the representative to act in a politically moderate fashion so as to attract as many voters from the middle of the ideological distribution. By moderating their voting behavior these representatives hope to capture Independents and moderate voters from both sides of the aisle. While this might please many voters from both political parties, it would also be a strategy in which many voters, very liberal Democrats and very conservative Republicans, remain largely unrepresented and dissatisfied with the way the representative votes. Regardless of which of these approaches the representative chooses to use, there are going to be voters who are not satisfied with the way that the MC votes. This is the key point—drawing heterogeneous districts leads to a less accurate form of representation. Fewer citizens in the district are satisfied with votes cast on the floor of the House by their MC.

One of the larger sticking points in the debate over the ratification of the Constitution was the ratio of representatives to constituents. Originally, the Constitution called for one representative in the House for every 30,000 people in a state. Thus if a state's population was 100,000 people according to the census, it would have three seats in the House. Representing 30,000 people is not easy and representing over 650,000 is an even more challenging task. We can try to make a representative's job easier by reducing the amount of diversity in a district, or we can make the job of representing a district impossible by maximizing the degree of diversity in a district. If we think of representation as reflecting citizens' point of view as accurately as possible, then we want to design a set of institutions that maximize this congruence. For instance, my ideal district is one with me and 649,999 people that think exactly like me. Such a constituency would see its wishes effectively translated into votes in Congress by their representative and the representative will remain faithful to the voters through the threat of a primary challenge. As we move away from the impossible ideal district, we can think about districts that minimize the ideological distance between voters and the likely representative. This fosters more effective representation and makes it easier for elected officials to discern our preferences. Downs provided social scientists with a theory of voting in which voters simply cast ballots based on the ideological proximity of the candidates.[8] Whichever candidate more closely represents our point of view receives our vote. I argue that we should take this notion of minimizing ideological distance not just as a theory of voting behavior, but rather as a way to improve the accuracy of representation. Thus, districts should be drawn so that the cumulative distance between the elected official and all voters in a district is minimized.

I demonstrated earlier that winning voters are systematically happier with their member of Congress in addition to being more satisfied with Congress as an institution. Instead of simply thinking of a packing partisan districting plan as making more people happy, I think a better conceptualization is that this increases the overall accuracy of representation, which, in turn, increases satisfaction with both the elected official and the institution as a whole, and these factors contribute to a more effective form of democracy.

Buchler develops this idea more formally and finds that homogeneous noncompetitive districts "do a better job than competitive districts in achieving representative outcomes."[9] He concludes, like I do in this work, that so-called bipartisan gerrymanders are actually much better in terms of the overall effectiveness of representation. He goes on to say that these districts "produce legislators that are closer to their district medians and more representative of everyone in their district."[10] Buchler is equally critical in his assessment of the ability of competitive elections to induce responsiveness among legislators.

The House of Representatives ought to be the closest of our national institutions to the people. We want the connection between the representative and the represented to be a close and faithful connection. The delegate theory of representation "posits that the representative ought to reflect purposively the preferences of his constituents."[11] Research on the connection between elected officials and the people that they represent has a long tradition in our discipline. Miller and Stokes's seminal piece on this subject called into question the ability of the representative to know what her constituents want, as well as the ability of the constituents to know and understand how the elected official is voting in Washington.[12]

For example, Miller and Stokes conclude: "The Representative has very imperfect information about the issue preferences of his constituency, and the constituency's awareness of the policy stands of the Representative ordinarily is slight."[13] While other scholars have pointed out some methodological concerns with the original Miller and Stokes study and have questioned the validity of some of their conclusions, there is very little doubt that these connections between the representative and the constituency could be much stronger.[14] Creating packed ideological districts will necessarily strengthen these bonds. If a Democrat is sent to Congress from a district heavily populated by like-minded partisans, she will have little doubt as to how her constituents prefer her to vote on policy proposals. Similarly, creating more "winners" out of voters alleviates some of the uncertainty with respect to how the representative votes on their behalf. This will also serve to encourage representatives to be more responsive to constituent needs.

## Packing districts prevents gerrymanders and leads to proportional outcomes

Redistricting is inherently political. The outcome of drawing electoral districts inevitably has very real political consequences by affecting the distribution of seats in Congress or the state legislature. Consider the following quote from the Supreme Court's decision in the *Gaffney v. Cummings* case:

> The very essence of districting is to produce a different—a more "politically fair"—result than would be reached with elections at large, in which the winning party would take 100 percent of the legislative seats. Politics and

political considerations are inseparable from districting and apportionment. The political profile of a State, its party registration, and voting
records are available precinct by precinct, ward by ward. These subdivisions
may not be identical with census tracts, but, when overlaid on a census
map, it requires no special genius to recognize the political consequences
of drawing a district line along one street rather than another. It is not
only obvious, but absolutely unavoidable, that the location and shape of
districts may well determine the political complexion of the area. District
lines are rarely neutral phenomena. They can well determine what district
will be predominantly Democratic or predominantly Republican, or make
a close race likely. Redistricting may pit incumbents against one another
or make very difficult the election of the most experienced legislator. The
reality is that districting inevitably has and is intended to have substantial
political consequences.
   (*Gaffney v. Cummings*, 412 U.S. 735 (1973) page 412 U.S. 735, 754).

And as redistricting is, in most states, left up to the state government, politicians are going to be looking out for their own interests and the interests of
fellow Democrats or Republicans. Some states have transferred the power of
districting to an outside body—these are often called "nonpartisan redistricting boards" or something of this ilk. Unfortunately, transferring the power to
draw districts does not leech the politics out of an inherently political process.
For instance, if a "nonpartisan" group is charged with instituting a new districting map, how are the members of this group chosen? Should it be a bunch
of retired judges? If so, then which judges? At some point someone else has
to make a decision as to who is on the board and who is not. If we let the
Democratic governor pick a handful of judges, what is to stop him from choosing only Democratic judges? The Supreme Court addressed this issue in the
following way:

> It may be suggested that those who redistrict and reapportion should
> work with census, not political, data and achieve population equality
> without regard for political impact. But this politically mindless approach
> may produce, whether intended or not, the most grossly gerrymandered
> results; and, in any event, it is most unlikely that the political impact of
> such a plan would remain undiscovered by the time it was proposed or
> adopted, in which event the results would be both known and, if not
> changed, intended.

While the shape of any district is going to have political implications, to what
extent should the map makers be able to extract as many seats for one party or
the other? It is natural for a party, either party, to take advantage of this process
to help their own candidates, but the question is to what extent should gerrymandering be allowed? The Supreme Court has sent mixed signals over the

constitutionality of partisan gerrymandering. Their first proclamation came in 1986 when they decided a case involving the state legislative district lines drawn in the state of Indiana after the 1980 census (*Davis v. Bandemer*). The case was brought by a group of Democratic legislators who did not care for the districts drawn by the Republicans (who controlled the state government, and therefore, the redistricting process at the time). This particular case involved strategic use of multimember districts by the Republicans to dilute the votes for Democratic candidates. For instance in the 1982 election for the state House of Representatives, Democratic candidates garnered 51.9 percent of votes cast statewide but only won 43 out of the 100 seats.

The majority opinion, written by Justice White, concluded that political gerrymandering was indeed justiciable (which is to say the Court can and should be involved in these kinds of cases) under the Equal Protection Clause. After deciding that these cases can be heard in a court of law, the Supreme Court was faced with outlining "manageable standards" for determining when a political gerrymander had indeed occurred.[15] The *Bandemer* decision has been heavily criticized over the years by academics and judges alike insofar as there is not a consensus as to what these standards are.

Reading the *Vieth v. Jubelirer* decision from 2004, there is little question that the *Bandemer* standards were useless. From Justice Scalia's plurality opinion:

> In her *Bandemer* concurrence, Justice O'Connor predicted that the plurality's standard "will over time either prove unmanageable and arbitrary or else evolve towards some loose form of proportionality." *Id.*, at 155 (opinion concurring in judgment, joined by Burger, C. J., and Rehnquist, J.). A similar prediction of unmanageability was expressed in Justice Powell's opinion, making it the prognostication of a majority of the Court. See *id.*, at 171 ("The . . . most basic flaw in the plurality's opinion is its failure to enunciate any standard that affords guidance to legislatures and courts"). That prognostication has been amply fulfilled.

Scalia goes on to quote various academics on the decision as well. Samuel Issacharoff writes "Bandemer only begot confusion."[16] Bernie Grofman is quoted as saying "[A]s far as I am aware I am one of only two people who believe that *Bandemer* makes sense. Moreover, the other person, Daniel Lowenstein, has a diametrically opposed view as to *what* the plurality opinion means."[17]

The standard from the *Bandemer* decision was that a political gerrymandering claim can succeed only where the plaintiffs show "both intentional discrimination against an identifiable political group and an actual discriminatory effect on that group." So there is an "intent prong" and an "effects prong" to this test, which is to say that a group suing in Court for relief must show that the map makers intended to discriminate against them (this can be problematic) and also show that the map had the effect to discriminate against them. This would be done by using a variety of historic factors and projected election results to show the group has been "denied its chance to effectively influence the political process" as a whole. This language is what turned out to be particularly problematic insofar as it is virtually impossible for one party to be denied its chance to influence the political process as a whole. While one group may not elect a Democratic to the House of Representatives, there may be a Democratic senator, or a Democratic governor, or even a Democratic president. Thus, the threshold set in the *Bandemer* case was so high as to prevent any group from ever being able to reach the threshold. While partisan gerrymandering was technically unconstitutional from 1986 onward, in reality there was not a single case brought before any court after this ruling where a judge found the facts sufficient to support reaching this threshold.

Issacharoff, Karlan, and Pildes put it this way: "[t]hroughout its subsequent history, *Bandemer* has served almost exclusively as an invitation to litigation without much prospect of redress."[18] In the entire history of cases brought before courts since the standards of *Bandemer* were set, not a single case involving political gerrymandering through the drawing of district lines was given relief by a judge. Or as Justice Scalia puts it: "The lower courts were set wandering in the wilderness for 18 years not because the *Bandemer* majority thought it a good idea, but because five Justices could not agree upon a single standard, and because the standard the plurality proposed turned out not to work" (plurality opinion in *Vieth v. Jubelirer*).

Successfully bringing a political gerrymandering case to Court was made even more difficult when the Court said that relying on a single election year for data analysis was not sufficient. Thus, new districts are drawn for the election of 2002, but no one can bring a case forward until after the 2004 election. At that time there were only three more elections to be held before lines were redrawn yet again. Moreover, the case had to wind through the various courts and any decision from a court below the Supreme Court can always be appealed. So it is an understatement to say that the litigation route may take several years to come to a resolution. At some point, rational actors in the process might simply conclude that waiting until the next round of redistricting makes more sense than trying to litigate the issue.

The issue of political gerrymandering was revisited by the Supreme Court in 2002 when a case involving the Pennsylvania congressional district lines was brought by Democrats in the state. The Republicans controlled the redistricting process in that state and drew a plan that was beneficial to their party. The Democrats naturally objected and sued in Court to have it overturned. Realizing that the *Bandemer* standards were unworkable, the Supreme Court vacated that particular decision. However, the conservative bloc on the Court was unable to convince Justice Kennedy to agree that courts should no longer hear political gerrymandering cases. Justices Scalia, Thomas, O'Connor, and Rehnquist were all on board to declare this issue nonjusticiable. None of these justices felt that there were "manageable standards" for detecting when a gerrymander has happened and they concluded that the *Bandemer* case was decided incorrectly. However, there was only a plurality opinion (four justices) and thus there is little precedential value in this decision.

Justice Kennedy, while agreeing that no such standards exist today, left the door cracked open for future claims with the prospect that a manageable standard may be created in the future. By withholding his vote from the plurality of conservative justices on the issue of justiciability, the Court can visit this issue in the future and, depending on the makeup of the Court at that time, further revise its opinion on whether or not gerrymandering is something that can be detected by the Court, and thus provide relief (i.e., strike the map down and force the state to redraw the map in such a way that it does not treat one party unfairly).

While the Court remains undecided as to whether or not it should be involved in partisan gerrymandering cases, it remains a huge problem in modern districting. One of the biggest benefits of a fair partisan approach with packed districts is that gerrymandering is nearly impossible. The number of Democrats and Republicans elected from a state will be largely determined by the number of Democratic and Republican voters in the state. Assuming that districts are drawn in a way that both parties are roughly equally packed, then each party will get the number of seats they "deserve" based on the proportion of people that vote or identify with that party. This is a good thing.

In the *Gaffney v. Cummings* case the Supreme Court has already put its stamp of approval on the approach advocated in this book. They term it the "political fairness" approach, but regardless of what it is called, it involves carving up the state into heavily Democratic or heavily Republican districts. A quote from the decision:

> The record abounds with evidence, and it is frankly admitted by those who prepared the plan, that virtually every Senate and House district line was drawn with the conscious intent to create a districting plan that would achieve a rough approximation of the statewide political strengths of the Democratic and Republican Parties, the only two parties in the State large enough to elect legislators from discernible geographic areas. Appellant insists that the spirit of "political fairness" underlying this plan is not only permissible, but a desirable consideration in laying out districts that otherwise satisfy the population standard of the reapportionment cases. Appellees, on the other hand, label the plan as nothing less than a gigantic political gerrymander, invidiously discriminatory under the Fourteenth Amendment.
>
> We are quite unconvinced that the reapportionment plan offered by the three-member Board violated the Fourteenth Amendment because it attempted to reflect the relative strength of the parties in locating and defining election districts. It would be idle, we think, to contend that any

political consideration taken into account in fashioning a reapportionment plan is sufficient to invalidate it.

(*Gaffney v. Cummings*, page 412 U.S. 735, 753)

The Court also addressed this in the *Bandemer* case:

> To draw district lines to maximize the representation of each major party would require creating as many safe seats for each party as the demographic and predicted political characteristics of the State would permit. This in turn would leave the minority in each safe district without a representative of its choice. We upheld this "political fairness" approach in *Gaffney v. Cummings*, despite its tendency to deny safe district minorities any realistic chance to elect their own representatives. But *Gaffney* in no way suggested that the Constitution requires the approach that Connecticut had adopted in that case.
>
> (*Davis v. Bandemer*, page 478 U.S. 109, 131–132)

## Competitive districting makes nonmajoritarian outcomes more likely

There are significant costs to drawing competitive districts. Knife-edge districts make "unfair" outcomes much more likely. If a district is equally divided between the two major parties, the candidates from each of these parties are susceptible to losing if a third party candidate emerges from their side of the ideological continuum. For instance, imagine 52 percent of a district prefers the Republican candidate to the Democratic candidate for the House seat in an upcoming election. A candidate for the Libertarian Party decides to run for the seat as well. If we assume that only voters on the far-right side of the ideological spectrum will vote for the Libertarian, then he need only pick up just over 4 percent of the vote to deny the Republican the seat (Democrat 48, Republican 47.9, and Libertarian 4.1).

The single-member district (SMD) system implies nonproportional outcomes, usually with the majority party receiving a larger than proportional share of the seats. The relationship between seats and votes in a SMD system is usually very responsive to shifts in the votes when the two political parties are fairly competitive. It also means that the party with the majority usually receives more than their proportional share of the seats. We can think of this as the "winner's bonus." So if the Democrats receive 55 percent of the votes statewide, it would not be remarkable if they won 60 percent of the seats in the same state. Robert Dahl (1998) recognizes this shortcoming in the SMD system.[19] He notes that "first past the post" (FPTP) systems can significantly misallocate seats among the parties due to the geographic spread of the votes across districts. If one party enjoys bare majority support across all the states, they would win every seat in the Senate. In the House we need to be even

more concerned since the "natural" spread of the parties' votes is less important since the electoral boundaries are fluid and changeable. He goes on to say
that "It is obvious, then, that in order for FPTP to result in acceptably fair
representation, party support must *not* be distributed evenly across a country.
Conversely, the more evenly voting support is distributed, the greater the
divergence between votes and seats will be. Thus, if regional differences decline
in a country, as appears to have been the case in Britain in 1997, the distortion
caused by FPTP grows."[20] The point that Dahl is making is the same one made
in chapter 1: FPTP with districts that are highly competitive (party support is
evenly spread) can lead to wildly unfair outcomes. Dahl says that as support is
more evenly spread, divergence will increase—this is not technically correct, as
it is possible for a purely competitive plan to result in proportional outcomes,
it just is not particularly likely to happen.

This nonproportional relationship between seats and votes of the SMD
system does not need to be treated as sacred or something that we ought to
exaggerate by allowing parties to pack and crack their opponents in a way that
deprives them of seats they might otherwise win. Instead of treating it as a
feature of the electoral system, let us treat it as a bug (i.e., something that can
and ought to be fixed). We can flatten out the seats–votes curve that usually
defines a SMD system by drawing fewer competitive districts. What little we
sacrifice in responsiveness we gain with outcomes that are more proportional
to the two parties, which is fairer to the voters in the state.

Congressional elections are plurality elections. This means the winner in
each district is simply the candidate with *the most* votes, and this need not be
a majority. If there are dozens of decent candidates running for a single seat,
the winner may in fact receive a very small proportion of the vote (10 percent,
5 percent, or even less).[21] Any candidate or candidates from minor parties that
can attract more than a trivial percentage of the vote can affect the outcome.
Thus, competitive districts are much more likely to lead to "unfair" outcomes
in which the candidate with less support than the other candidate wins only
because a minor party candidate emerges. To make matters worse, when a
decent third party candidate does emerge and goes on to lose the election, the
most likely outcome is that the candidate actually cost the candidate from
the closer party, in terms of ideology, the election. We witnessed this first hand
in the 2000 presidential election in Florida. I am personally convinced that the
butterfly-style ballot in Palm Beach County did cost Al Gore the election—the
most reliable estimates are that roughly 2,000 would-be Gore voters accidentally voted for Pat Buchanan.[22] Since President Bush's margin of victory
was only 537 votes, this would have been sufficient to change the election
outcome. Even more so than the famed butterfly ballot is the number of votes
that Ralph Nader attracted as the Green Party candidate. He polled 97,488
votes in the state of Florida alone. If we (safely) assume that more than half of
these voters would have cast a ballot for Al Gore rather than George W. Bush,
then this too changes the election outcome. Thus, Al Gore loses the presidency

even though most voters in Florida preferred Gore to Bush for president, but when a left-wing party runs a quality candidate that attracts votes, the Democratic candidate suffers and we end up with a nonmajoritarian outcome.

Both major parties are fully aware of the danger that minor party candidates can play in close states or districts. This leads to further ugliness and hardball politics. For instance, after the 2000 presidential election the last thing the Democratic Party wanted was an encore performance by Ralph Nader in 2004. To that end, the Democrats did their best to keep Nader out of the race, at first by pleading with him to stay out. They appealed to him that they all shared at least one basic goal—to get Bush out of the White House. When this did not work and Nader decided to pursue the presidency as a candidate of the Green Party, the Democrats resorted to rather undemocratic means of keeping Nader's impact to a minimum.[23] In the state of Arizona, Governor Janet Napolitano (D) and the Democratic Party successfully kept Mr. Nader off the ballot in Arizona in the hopes that John Kerry could beat George W. Bush in that state (unfortunately for the Democrats, even without Nader on the ballot, Kerry still lost). The Nader campaign needed to qualify for the general election ballot by gathering the signatures of about 15,000 registered voters in the state. When the petitions were turned in, the Democrats challenged the validity of thousands of signatures on these petitions and filed a lawsuit. Eventually, the Nader campaign gave up on Arizona and conceded that there were technical problems with the petitions. While clearly the Democrats were well within the letter of the law in their challenge to the Nader campaign, and given the reaction of the Nader campaign, he should not have been on the ballot, nonetheless the point is that this approach to electioneering is not particularly democratic, nor is it reassuring to the American public when the entrenched parties work so hard to keep other candidates from simply appearing on the ballot.

While there is nothing we can do about statewide elections and the impact that third party candidates may play in competitive elections there, we can do something about congressional and state legislative districts. Again, the moral of the story here is that competitive districts are highly vulnerable to outcomes in which the candidate with the most support actually loses. This is not true in packed districts where the real competition will occur in the primary election as opposed to the general election, which in most districts will not play a critical role in determining who represents the district.

## Votes are hard to count

Ever since the 2000 election and the vote counting boondoggle in Florida, Americans have been more in tune to the fact that counting votes turns out to be much more difficult that it sounds. If voters punch cards, as they did in many states around the country in 2000, sometimes the voter does not punch the spot hard enough to punch the "chad" out of the appropriate spot.

Sometimes a voter might punch too many spots on the card and spoil his ballot. Sometimes the ballot is so poorly designed that some people will punch the card in the wrong spot, voting for a candidate that they did not intend to vote for. This is exactly what happened in Palm Beach County, Florida in the 2000 election where they used the "butterfly ballot," which listed candidates on both sides of a center line of holes, where the voter was to punch the ballot. The ballot design was confusing because of the staggered nature of the ballot. On the top of the left side of the ballot was George W. Bush, while Al Gore was just below Bush on the left side of the ballot. At the top of the ballot on the right hand side was the Reform Party candidate Patrick Buchanan. So if a voter preferred Bush, she punched the top hole; a punch in the second hole was a vote for Buchanan, while the third spot indicated a voter cast a ballot for Gore. If a voter simply looked at the left hand side of the ballot, she quickly saw the two major party candidates and if she preferred Gore to Bush she might very well simply punch the second hole from the top, even though the ballot indicated with a small arrow to punch the third hole down for Gore. Buchanan ended up receiving far more votes proportionally in this county than in any other in the state of Florida. Reasonable estimates have at least 2,000 would-be Gore voters accidentally casting their ballot for Buchanan.[24]

Bush ended up beating Gore in Florida by less than 700 votes, so this poorly designed ballot could easily have been decisive. This leads directly into the next point. Elections decided by a small number of votes can easily be decided incorrectly because counting ballots is not easy and is not done without mistakes. Thus, the final tally of ballots is just an estimate of the true preferences of all the voters who cast their ballot. For a variety of reasons, ballots get spoiled and preferences are not recorded with 100 percent accuracy. Assume for the sake of this argument that one percent of ballots are spoiled, disqualified, lost, or somehow not counted. The closer the election, the more important this inaccuracy becomes. Indeed, if the election is decided by less than one percentage point then without the true preferences of the ballots that were spoiled, we do not actually know who really won the election. As Buchler says about the butterfly ballot in Florida—"[It] would have been irrelevant if the election had not been so close."[25]

Since the problems in Florida, the country has been set on a path of trying to improve voting technology. The federal government even passed a law, the Help America Vote Act (HAVA). The bill passed in the House 347–48 and 92–2 in the Senate and was signed into law by President Bush on October 29, 2002. It provided billions of dollars, in an effort to replace old voting technologies, to try to alleviate some of the problems associated with the 2000 election. Changing to computerized voting or mail-in balloting is not going to make this problem go away. The fact of the matter is that any method of recording preferences is not foolproof and therefore votes will be lost. We should really think of the final count in any election as merely an estimate and the closer the election, the less certain we can be about who the winner really is.

Imagine if every election were decided by a single vote—we have essentially thrown democracy into the wind since each election will be ultimately decided by the distribution of spoiled ballots and miscounted votes. If uncounted votes break perfectly evenly, then the outcome is correct. This is unlikely to be the case. So then we are left with two possible outcomes, the first of which is not all that bad—the "winning" candidate had more spoiled ballots than the loser—so while the winner really won by a larger margin, we can at least be satisfied that the correct man or woman has been put into office. The second outcome, which is a priori just as likely as the first outcome, is one where the "losing" candidate had a larger share of the spoiled ballots, miscounted votes, and uncounted votes. Here the outcome is quite sinister—the wrong person is selected to the office.

## Conclusion

A packed partisan plan for redistricting improves how well citizens are represented in Congress or in their state legislatures which, in turn, improves their attitudes toward these governments. General elections will not be particularly exciting under this approach, but we are not trying to maximize the entertainment value of elections. Elections are about translating what the people want into who gets elected into office and into public policies that they support, not about an election hinging on a single vote. Or multiple recounts of ballots and the inevitable court case to follow. Counting ballots is a difficult thing to do and the closer the margin of the election, the less likely the "correct" person is put into office. Minor party candidates can be spoilers in general elections, which leads to the election of someone who is not the more preferred candidate by the voters. A fair partisan approach improves representation by creating districts with less ideological variance among the constituents. This makes translating what the constituents want into votes by a representative more manageable and easier. It is impossible to escape the fact that the more diverse the district, the worse a representative will do in terms of giving the constituents what they want.

# Chapter 6

# Addressing the critiques

There is no doubt that changing the outlook among voters, scholars, elected officials, and the media with respect to the utility of competitive general elections and redistricting in the way that I suggest here will not be a trivial task. The notion of the need for competitive general elections is deeply rooted in our national psyche. Moreover, I suspect many people think that the district maps that exist today already look a great deal like the kind I propose in this book. Many states, such as California, created what political scientists call a "bipartisan gerrymander" in which the map is drawn in such a way as to protect all incumbents, both Democrats and Republicans, which minimizes the number of competitive districts. However, many of these districts still "waste" a significant number of votes. A district that is 65 percent Democratic is fairly safe, but over one-third of the voters will still be dissatisfied with the election outcome (in this case all the Republicans). I am advocating trimming the number of Republicans in this type of district further still. To say that this proposal is provocative is an understatement. The overwhelming sentiment in the country seems to be that we need more competition in these elections, and certainly not less. My point is that the common wisdom has it backwards, and in this chapter I address some of the common criticisms of the approach that I am advocating.

## Polarization and redistricting

In recent years political observers and social scientists have documented the increasing polarization of the two American political parties in Congress. While the evidence for this polarization is quite clear, scholars have not come to a definitive conclusion as to what is the root cause for this development. The media however, have come to a conclusion and the following quote is typical:

> American elections are growing ever less competitive while squeezing out moderates from both parties and polarizing politics. This is in part because politicians get to choose their voters, rather than the reverse, and

so they draw districts that are reliably Republican or Democratic. The system corrodes democracy.[1]

Underlying this quote is the following causal logic: (1) Increases in average district homogeneity can be linked to changes in redistricting practices that make it more likely that politically homogeneous districts will be drawn. In particular, in each decade from the 1960s through the 1990s, an increasing number of majority–minority districts have been drawn as a result of actions taken under Section 2 and Section 5 of the Voting Rights Act of 1965 (as amended in 1982). Such districts pack voters with similar characteristics and predilections into a single district, while bleaching neighboring districts of minority voters and loyal Democrats, still further increasing average levels of district homogeneity. More generally, the post-*Reynolds v. Sims* focus on "one person, one vote" as an overriding factor has meant that districts need no longer be drawn entirely within existing political subunit boundaries— boundaries which often include somewhat heterogeneous populations. This process of "fine-tuned" gerrymandering is greatly facilitated by the new computer GIS (geographic information systems) technology. Thus, the potential for artful partisan gerrymandering, where the party in control of the process packs its opponents voting strength into a limited number of districts while creating safe districts for its own candidates, has been increased. On the other hand, the potential for carefully crafted bipartisan gerrymanders that are effectively sweetheart deals with safe seats for incumbents of both parties has also been increased. The proliferation of these plans has prompted many critics to charge that voters are not selecting elected officials, but politicians are selecting their voters.

(2) Reductions in the levels of district competition are caused (at least in large part) by increases in average district homogeneity, because homogeneous districts tend to be highly uncompetitive. However, now that regional realignments have more or less sorted themselves out (the Northeast has far fewer moderate Republicans and the South has far fewer moderate Democrats), the distinctiveness of the two major parties is clearer (to both candidates and voters) than it has been in decades. This makes is quite difficult for one party to win a district that leans toward the other party.

(3) Increases in political polarization are caused by declines in political competition, because representatives from safe seats can more easily disregard the views of minority party voters in their constituencies without fear of repercussions than can representatives from marginal seats. Thus, representatives from these seats will look more like the median or modal party member from their own party than like the overall median in their district (or in the nation as a whole). Moreover, even if the standard Downsian story were correct, and the representative would resemble the overall median voter, in a homogeneous district that median voter will be much more of an ideological extremist than would be the case in a more closely politically divided

constituency. Furthermore, the candidates who win in the primaries tend to be less moderate in these kinds of districts. There are far fewer "moderates" from either side of the aisle and those that do run might be having a tougher time winning now that the parties are more clearly sorted ideologically.[2]

This often repeated relationship is wrong. Most of the scholarship on this topic virtually exonerates redistricting as the cause for increased polarization in the electorate. Brunell and Grofman (2008) show that while redistricting since the 1960s has decreased diversity in congressional districts, the next two links in the chain are wrong.[3] Homogenous districts are not necessarily uncompetitive and members elected from safe districts by large margins are no more ideologically polarized that members elected in highly competitive affairs. Ono finds that "although elections and voters most likely play a role in the polarization of House members in some form, redistricting has little to do with it."[4] One piece of suggestive evidence that redistricting is not the culprit is that when you compare the ideological distribution of House members and Senators over the past 40 years or so, it is clear that polarization has occurred, but this separation of the two parties is evident in both the House and the Senate. Since the Senate's electoral boundaries never change, it is hard to imagine that redistricting is to blame for this development in the House and that some other exogenous force can explain the polarization in the Senate.[5]

There is some research suggesting that redistricting is at the very least partially the cause of polarization. Theriault tries to quantify how much of the polarization that has taken place over the last three decades can be attributed to redistricting.[6] Using a variety of tests he does find some evidence that redistricting is at least partially to blame for polarization (for instance, new House members are more extreme (polarized) than new Senators). He concludes that somewhere between 10 and 25 percent of the polarization may be caused by redistricting.

The concern here is that if the members of Congress who face no real general election competition tend to be much further to the left or right than members who are not in safe districts, then this type of redistricting plan would further polarize an already extremely partisan House of Representatives. The common wisdom suggests that bipartisan redistricting plans that protect all current incumbents by drawing safe districts for both parties, allows these members to more or less ignore Independents and moderate voters in the district. The net effect then is that the aggregate representation in the House of Representatives would not accurately reflect the views of the voters.

This leaves us with a relatively straightforward empirical question: what is the relationship between the margin of victory and a congressperson's ideology? As political parties also figure prominently in the discussion of ideology, we will also discuss the impact of party as well. We hypothetically explore what effect these two variables have, if any, on the ideology of MCs. Figures 6.1–6.4 represent four hypothetical relationships between these two independent

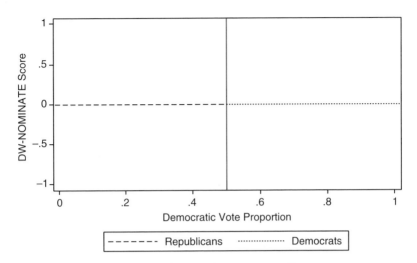

*Figure 6.1* Hypothetical no party effect or election margin effect.

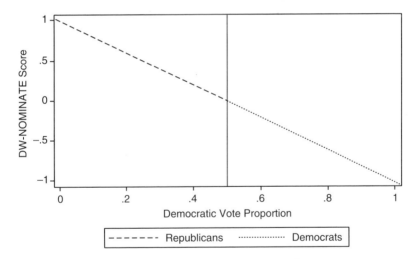

*Figure 6.2* Hypothetical election margin effect but no party effect.

variables and the dependent variable. The vertical axis represents ideology (denoted by DW-NOMINATE scores, a well-known measure of ideology in the U.S. Congress). This variable ranges from +1 (very conservative) to −1 (very liberal). The horizontal axis represents the proportion of the vote received by the Democratic candidate. This variable ranges from 0 (the Republican received 100 percent of the vote) to 1 (the Democrat received 100 percent of the vote). Republicans are those data points to the left of the vertical line at .5 and Democrats are to the right of this line.

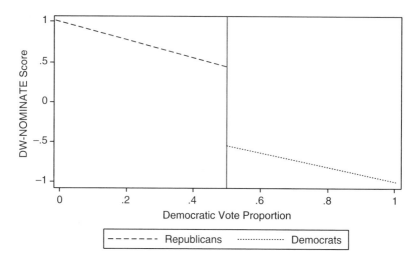

*Figure 6.3* Hypothetical party effect and election margin effect.

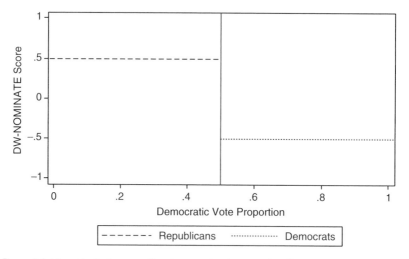

*Figure 6.4* Hypothetical party effect but no election margin effect.

In Figure 6.1 there is no effect of either party or margin of victory. The graph is simply a straight horizontal line indicating that all members of Congress have, on average, the same ideology. Republicans are the same as Democrats and the margin of victory has no effect within or between the parties.

Figure 6.2 is what the data might look like if there is no party effect but there is a margin of victory effect. The line slopes downward from left to right indicating that as the Democratic proportion of the vote goes up, the ideology score goes down (from conservative to liberal). However, there is no discontinuity between the parties, so if a Republican wins by 1 vote he will be just trivially more conservative than a Democrat who wins by 1 vote. In other words, the two lines have the same slope and they meet right in the middle, so for each additional vote for the Democrat, the Representative gets just a bit more liberal regardless of whether the representative is a Democrat or Republican.

Figure 6.3 is the hypothetical representation if there is both a party effect and a margin of victory effect. The line slopes downward from left to right indicating that as the Democrat (Republican) receives more (fewer) votes, the member of Congress that is elected becomes more liberal (and less conservative). So a Republican that wins 80–20 is more conservative than a Republican that wins 60–40, and so on. Furthermore, there is a discontinuity or a jump in the data as we transition from Republicans (to the left of the vertical line) to Democrats (to the right of the line). So a narrow victory for a Democrat produces a member who is, on average, significantly more liberal than a Republican who wins by an equally small margin.

Finally, in Figure 6.4 the data shows what we might expect if there is a party effect, but no effect from the margin of victory. Here all Republicans are just as conservative as all other Republicans and all Democrats are as liberal as all the other Democrats. Within the parties there is no difference with respect to ideology regardless of the margin of victory. There are marked differences between the two parties though.

If safer seats, which have large margins of victory, lead to more polarized members of Congress, then the actual data should look something like Figure 6.2 or 6.3. If there is no effect between margin of victory and the degree of ideological polarization, then the actual data might resemble Figure 6.1 or 6.4.

Figure 6.5 plots the ideology of members of the House of Representatives by vote percentage for the years 1952–2000. The x-axis represents the Democratic proportion of the vote, so very small values indicate Republican victors by very large margins. The closer one moves toward the vertical line at .5, the more competitive the elections. The data on the far right side of the graph (those data points near 1.0) are districts in which the Democrat won by very large margins. The solid line is the predicted values from a quadratic regression and the shaded regions represent the 95 percent confidence region. The predicted lines look a great deal like the hypothetical relationship in Figure 6.4 in which there is a party effect (Democrats are more liberal than Republicans) but no margin of victory effect. The predicted line to the left of the vertical line which separates Republicans from Democrats is flat—thus, a Republican is a Republican irrespective of the margin of victory. For the Democrats the line is for the most part flat with a slight upward turn at the far right side of the graph.[7] The trend for Democrats is that as the margin of victory increases, a Democrat tends to be more *conservative*. This upward shift is driven largely by the uncontested elections in which a Democrat gets 100 percent of the votes.

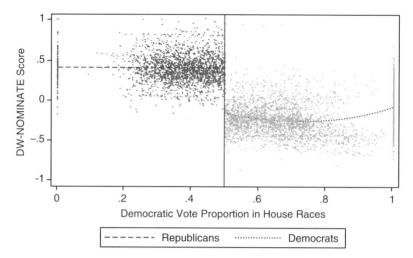

*Figure 6.5* The relationship between margin of victory and ideology in the House.

The graph depicts the quadratic regression line for DW-NOMINATE scores regressed on margin of victory (done separately for Democrats and Republicans). The vertical line at .5 separates Republicans (to the left of the line) from Democrats (to the right of the line). The sample sizes for the regression models are 4,627 for Republicans and 6,318 for Democrats.

Many of these data points are old Southern Democrats who tended to be fairly conservative.

There exists some evidence to support the argument that electoral competition leads to policy moderation among members of Congress. Ansolabehere, Snyder, and Stewart use data from the 1996 election and show that among other variables, as a district's preferences for the Republican presidential candidate move toward 50 percent (i.e., parity with the Democratic candidate), the ideological gap between the two candidates for the House seat decreases on average.[8] While this is suggestive of a relationship, it is important to note that first, they did not measure competitiveness of the House election directly (using actual House election outcomes) and second they find that challenges in primary elections also serve to close this gap. Thus, competition in a primary election, absent serious competition in the general election, may still serve to moderate the ideology of incumbent members of Congress. A hard fought race between two candidates from the same party will foster discussion among candidates and voters just like a closely fought election between candidates from different parties. There is nothing fundamental to the principles of democracy that requires competitive general elections. To the extent that competitiveness is healthy, we can substitute competitiveness at the primary election stage for competition in the general election.

The conclusion to take away from this exercise is that artificially creating more safe seats should not impact the degree of liberalness or conservativeness in elected members of Congress (and making current safe seats even safer ought not effect ideology on average either). The trend toward polarization is not due to redistricting, and creating even more fully packed districts will not impact polarization. Thus, there is no reason to expect that a multitude of members from districts that have noncompetitive general elections will lead to any dysfunctional aspects that impede the chamber's ability to pass good and representative legislation. Indeed, as I argued earlier, I think members representing homogenous constituencies should have an easier time inferring what their voters prefer, which should lead to legislation that is more representative of the country as a whole.

## Responsiveness of individual members of Congress

One of the bigger and more important fears with respect to a packed districting plan is that incumbents who do not need to fear competition in the general election will not be responsive to their constituents and may even become corrupt. Since incumbents are virtually guaranteed reelection (in the general election) they will not necessarily have to do as their constituents wish. For instance, in an amicus brief to the Supreme Court on the Texas redistricting case in 2006, some eminent scholars wrote: "The Elections Clause does not empower state legislatures artificially to create overwhelmingly noncompetitive congressional districting plans whose purpose and effect is overwhelmingly to insulate preferred candidates from electoral accountability."[9] This line of reasoning is misguided in my mind. General election competitiveness is not the key to keeping elected officials accountable, since as long as incumbents are uncertain about their chances of getting reelected, they will respond to the preferences of their constituents. We do not need to maximize this uncertainty by forcing incumbents to run the gauntlet of a competitive primary election *and* a competitive general election; indeed, it is not necessary for either election to be competitive at all. Rather, it is the *potential* for an incumbent to face a tough challenge in an election and lose the seat that is important to ensure responsive representation.

Representatives who act or vote in a way that is not congruent with their constituency clearly pose problems for democratic theory. The foundation for the Republican form of government is that the people elect representatives to act on their behalf, where voters authorize a single person to vote for them and remain accountable to them. When the elected official casts a vote that is *not* in the interests of his constituency, social scientists call this lack of faithfulness "shirking." The term is derived from shirking one's duty to act in a specific way. Interestingly, but not surprising in my mind, the extant literature finds almost no evidence of shirking in the modern Congress in any meaningful way.[10] One instance in which we might fully expect representatives to shirk is when they are certain that they are not running for reelection. They are free from the electoral connection that keeps them faithful and are free to do as they please. Opponents of term limits regularly invoke this argument to buttress their point of view—if members are forbidden from being reelected, then in their last term they are free to act and vote how they wish. Rothenberg and Sanders address this very point.[11] They examine the voting behavior of members who have voluntarily decided to leave the House and find that in the last few months of the term these members shirk both on an ideological dimension (i.e., their voting behavior changes) and on an abstention dimension (i.e., they participate less often). However, Carson et al. re-analyze these data and find that once proper control variables are put in the equation these effects disappear.[12] Drawing districts with very little ideological diversity will not increase shirking. Members of the House will remain faithful to their constituents. Indeed, as I argued earlier, members will be more representative because of the homogeneity—since their districts are so homogeneous there is very little uncertainty about what the preferences of the constituents are.

Clearly faithfulness or responsiveness is central to any theory of representation. So the question is: what keeps members responsive to the people? The keystone for responsiveness is clearly elections. The routine and regular consultation of the people through elections is the central mechanism for this faithfulness. How exactly do elections serve this purpose though? I argue that elections inculcate some degree of *uncertainty* as to whether or not the representative will be able to keep her job. A seat in the House of Representatives is rather valuable. It is a good job with a great deal of power and prestige, and while the member will not get rich on the salary, neither will he be particularly poor. The threat of losing this valued position via the electoral process is quite real. When thinking about this, one really needs to try to imagine being in a similar situation to members of the House of Representatives. You have a really nice job with great benefits, a reasonably attractive salary, and a significant amount of power. This is a job that people want to get and keep. In order to keep this job you need to win more votes than any other candidate in your district every two years. Fenno said it best: members of Congress are "fraught with uncertainty" when it comes to getting reelected.[13] This uncertainty stems from a variety of sources: Will your core supporters turnout to vote on Election Day? Have you done right by your district? What votes in the House will your opponent use against you in the campaign? Did you raise enough money for the campaign? Did you run your campaign properly? I suspect election night is a rather nervous time for most elected officials, even those that have been routinely reelected to office for decades.

Thus, it is not necessary for the general election to actually be competitive, which would certainly heighten the uncertainty for the incumbent, to have the electoral process instill the sense of need for the MC to represent his reelection constituency effectively. It is merely the threat of removal that instills this uncertainty. This is one of the reasons that people who oppose term limits rely on to make their point. If term limits are put in place, then each elected official will, at some point, be it two terms or six terms, a lame duck. If someone cannot be reelected, then there is no uncertainty about what will happen at the end of the term—that person is leaving office. Limiting terms then may change opportunity structures for representatives in such a way that they will lack the appropriate motivation to be faithful to the district in their last term in office.

There is empirical evidence that this link is particularly weak. Cleary studied the relationship between electoral competition and responsiveness in Mexico and found no connection between the two. He writes: "anecdotal and case study evidence suggests that many politicians in Mexico are hard working, competent, and effective. But electoral competition does not make them more so."[14] While Cleary attributes the lack of a connection to institutional features of Mexican elections, such as the inability of incumbents to run for reelection, it is not clear to me that given some different set of electoral institutions we would expect this connection either.

Therefore the linchpin for keeping representatives responsive to their constituents is the existence of some amount of uncertainty in the representative's own mind about whether or not he will be reelected by the voters in his district. While this uncertainty is clearly significantly higher when districts are drawn in such a way as to maximize competitiveness, it is not clear that it is necessary for the election to be competitive for the representative to experience this uncertainty. I am not the first person to make this argument. David Mayhew wrote: "It is possible to conceive of an assembly in which no member ever comes close to losing a seat but in which the need to be reelected is what inspires members' behavior. It would be an assembly with no saints or fools in it, an assembly packed with skilled politicians going about their business."[15] It is the potential to lose an election, not the degree to which someone experiences nearly losing an election that keeps representatives on their toes.

While the number of incumbents who actually run for reelection and lose is typically very small, the fact that some incumbents do get beat serves as notice to the other incumbents that it could happen to them as well.[16] For instance, in 2004, Phil Crane, the Republican incumbent from the Illinois eighth congressional district, lost his bid for reelection. This is important because Phil Crane was first elected to Congress in 1969 (in a special election to replace Donald Rumsfeld who had left for a position in the Nixon Administration). Crane then went on to be reelected 16 consecutive times. In 2004 he was the longest serving Republican in the entire House of Representatives. So he had clearly built up a reputation in his district. Even more interesting is that Crane's district was one of the most heavily Republican congressional districts in all of Illinois.[17] How did Crane manage to lose this seat? Media reports suggest that he just did not campaign that hard in the general election, which allowed newcomer Melissa Bean to win the seat. The important part of the story is that all of Phil's former colleagues that did win reelection know what happened to him. Incumbents know that complacency can cost them their seat in the House and this fear keeps members on their toes in terms of satisfying the voters in the district.

American congressional elections use a two-stage election system in which a candidate must first win a spot on the general election ballot by winning her party's primary election. The organized political parties in America do not, as they do in most other countries, simply put all candidates on the ballot. Candidates must win a plurality election in the district to earn a spot on the general election ballot. Thus, a redistricting plan with packed districts does not remove competitiveness altogether, but rather switches the locus of competition from the general election stage to the primary election stage, from *inter*-party competition to *intra*-party competition. Even if it were possible to draw a district that had no Republican voters whatsoever, we would not expect the Democrat to be insulated from the wishes of her constituents since there is still a mechanism for removing the Representative in the primary election. Surely, general elections under this kind of redistricting scheme would be rather uneventful and boring, but primary elections can be decisive. In fact we would expect most of the replacement of representatives to happen at the primary stage.

While modern primary elections are typically spectacularly uncompetitive affairs, there is no reason for it to remain this way. Instead of focusing our attention on getting out the vote only in the general election, political parties and interest groups can encourage people to turn out and vote in the primary election as well. This would almost certainly happen to some degree when the primary election is decisive. Indeed, there is some evidence that as the primary election becomes more important, for instance in one-party states, turnout in the primary relative to the general election increases.[18] Jewell and Sigelman find that "people are most likely to vote in primary elections if they perceive the primaries to be competitive, although this relationship is not extremely strong. We have also found, as we expected, that voters are more likely to vote in primaries if they live in a county where their party is dominant."[19] So when primaries count, people do turnout in larger numbers. Primaries can also be decisive—for instance, in the 2006 primary election season there were three high-profile incumbents who were defeated by members of their own party. More notable among these three was Joe Lieberman (D-CT) who was unseated by a Democrat from the left. Lieberman was criticized as being too cozy with President Bush and many voters in Connecticut were unhappy with Senator Lieberman's stance on the war in Iraq. Two House incumbents were also beat in primaries: Cynthia McKinney (D-GA) and Joe Schwarz (R-MI). McKinney was a lightning rod for controversy including various run-ins with the media and Capitol Hill police.

There are also aspects of packed districts that make running for Congress more attractive for high-quality candidates. First, as districts become more homogenous, candidates are more assured that they will not face a tough race in the general election. Thus, there is only one election to raise money for, campaign for, and win. Second, one of the biggest reasons that primary elections in America are so uncompetitive at the moment is because the organized political parties do not get involved in primary elections all that much. Even if the Republican Party does not particularly like Republican representative X, they are not going to try to beat him in the primary election because then they risk losing the seat altogether. While the evidence from the political science literature is really mixed on whether primary divisiveness actually decreases the chances of a general election win in a congressional seat,[20] the political parties clearly think that it might (i.e. there is enough uncertainty there to make parties act to preserve the seats that they have). The tougher the primary election, the less likely a candidate will win the general election. If they bloody up their own incumbent in a tough primary, a political party is actually decreasing the likelihood that the seat will continue to be controlled by one of their own. However, if districts are drawn so that one party is the overwhelming favorite to win the general election, this alleviates the concern about losing the seat to the opposing party in the general election, which opens the door for the party to become more involved at the primary stage. And even if primary elections remain rather uncompetitive, that does not mean that this alleviates the uncertainty from the mind of the incumbent, and it is this modicum of uncertainty that is necessary to keep an elected official responsive to the district.

Critics of modern redistricting practices routinely refer to the process as one in which incumbents pick their voters rather than voters picking members of Congress. Describing the redistricting process in rather bold terms, North Carolina State Senator Mark McDaniel has said: "We are in the business of rigging elections."[21] This attitude naturally does not alleviate the public's attitudes toward elected officials and the redistricting process. However, there is nothing inherently wrong with an elected official representing a homogeneous, and presumably a safe, district. The absence of competition in the general election is not detrimental to democracy, and trying to increase the number of competitive state legislative or congressional general elections is not a panacea for any problems, real or perceived.

Going back to the hypothetical example in chapter 1 (Figure 1.1) where we have two methods of redistricting—hyper-competitive and hyper-safe districts—the traditional argument from political scientists and the media is that increased competition has a positive effect on responsiveness. The more likely an incumbent is to lose, the more the representative is going to do what the people want. Now imagine being a representative in a truly 50–50 hyper-competitive district. It is impossible to be responsive to *all* of your constituents. Why? Because the constituency does not agree among itself how a representative should vote on a bill, they are divided. Competitive districts are, by definition, ideologically divided districts. From the outset it is impossible to be responsive to the entire district. This representative might be very responsive to a portion of the district, but he cannot represent a significant portion of the district given the way in which the district was drawn.

Responsiveness and representation boil down to how well the representative reflects the views of her district. Representation is a single person trying to reflect the views of an aggregation of individuals and we can thus evaluate the extent to which a representative is doing a good or accurate job by measuring the proportion of those being represented who are pleased with how the legislator votes. Thus, *ceteris paribus*, the more ideological variance that exists within a constituency, the less accurate the representation can be. A member of a legislature can vote either "aye" or "nay" on any given bill, but if half the district prefers "aye" and the other wants a "nay," it is impossible to accurately reflect any more than half the voters. If we continue to insist on drawing competitive districts, then we are necessarily excluding the possibility that more people get their views represented in Congress. Homogeneous districts make it more likely that voters are pleased with the votes cast by the member of Congress, so representation is more accurate and responsiveness is higher. So while common wisdom suggests that competitive elections tend to increase responsiveness of elected officials, it should be clear now that quite the opposite is true—the higher the ideological variance within a district, the *less* possible it is for the member to be responsive.

Will the member of Congress do other things to try to increase the likelihood of getting reelected? Of course, but these activities typically include things such as securing pork barrel projects for the district, or completing more case work on the behalf of constituents. So if by responsiveness we mean getting more earmarked projects or helping people navigate the bureaucracy, then more competition might mean more responsiveness. However, if we are interested in a notion of representation of a higher order, and I think we are, or at the very least we should be, then responsiveness is more accurately measured in terms of what proportion of the constituency is happy with the votes that the member cast on the floor of the House on the most important issues of the day.

## Responsiveness of the electoral system

There are a variety of metrics that have been designed or discovered over the years that are useful for evaluating different electoral systems. For instance, various scholars are interested in why some countries have more political parties than others and what impact differing electoral systems have on how many parties emerge. This stems back to Duverger's Law and the distinction between proportional representation (PR) systems (with multiple parties) and single-member district (SMD) systems (which encourages two parties). Laakso and Taagepera developed a simple metric to calculate what they call the "effective number of parties" because just counting any political party that claims to exist or that may have received a handful of votes does not make much sense.[22] Beyond measuring how many parties, social scientists are also interested in the relationship between seats and votes and how changes in the proportion of votes for a party gets translated into a change in the proportion of seats in the legislature. Scholars call this metric the "swing ratio" or the "responsiveness" of the electoral system.

The swing ratio captures the degree to which aggregate swings in the vote proportion are translated into shares of the seats in the legislature.[23] The more responsive the electoral system (the higher the swing ratio), the more seats a party will earn in the legislature for an increase in their share of the votes nationwide. For instance, in a PR system, used in many countries around the world, parties are awarded seats in parliament equal to their overall share of the votes.[24] In a nationwide party list PR system, there are no districts per se, but rather the country is one single district. Parties put out a "party list" of would-be members of the parliament and they campaign for votes nationwide. Then if the Green Party gets 15 percent of the vote nationwide, they will receive 15 percent of the seats in the national legislature. In this type of electoral system the swing ratio is equal to 1.[25] If the Green Party increases its share of the vote from 15 percent to 18 percent, their share of the seats will increase from 15 percent to 18. Thus, PR has a 1-to-1 correspondence of votes and seats, which yields a swing ratio of 1. Single-member district systems have a more complicated relationship between seats and votes, but the swing ratio in these systems is almost always higher than the swing ratio of PR systems.

Figure 6.6 represents a generalized relationship between seats and votes for both a SMD system and a PR system. The curve for SMD system is often called

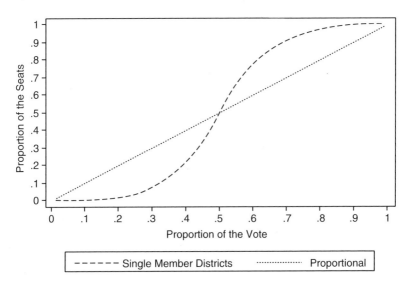

*Figure 6.6* Seats–votes curves for single member district and proportional representation.

an "S-curve" given its shape. When Party A receives 20 percent of the vote (and the other party then receives 80 percent), Party A can expect to receive a very small proportion of the votes (approaching zero). Furthermore, if Party A increases its vote share to 21 percent of the vote, they are still going to receive roughly zero seats in the legislature.[26] However, when the two parties are more competitive with one another (they both have around 50 percent of the vote), then small increases in their vote totals nationwide have a disproportionate effect on their seats totals. For instance, the slope of the line in the region where each party commands half the vote (.5) is roughly 3. So if the swing ratio is 3, this means that if either party manages to pick up an extra 1 percent of the vote nationwide, we expect them to receive an additional 3 percent of the seats in the House of Representatives. While this value varies from year to year over the last 30 years or so, it averages about 2.[27]

The relatively high levels of responsiveness in single-member district systems is related to having at least some seats that are in the competitive range. In order for one party to realize a 3 percent gain in seats from a 1 percent gain in the vote, there has to be a number of seats that were vulnerable to being taken away from the other party. One can imagine that if every seat in the House of Representatives were drawn so that each district has near parity in the number of voters, that a very small shift in the vote nationwide (i.e., affecting voters in all districts the same way) could have huge effects in the number or seats that each party controls. Using an extreme example, we could imagine a small shift in one election delivering all 435 seats to the Democrats and two years later a small shift rightward in the electorate delivering every seat to the GOP. On the other hand, if virtually all of the seats are drawn to minimize competitiveness, then aggregate changes in the vote totals would have little to no effect on the division of seats in the House between the two political parties. Said differently, the plan I have advocated in this book would flatten out the S-curve of a typical single-member district system and the proportion of seats that each party receives would not change much with modest or significant changes in the two parties' shares of the vote nationwide. So if we pack districts with say 80 percent Democrats (or Republicans), then the division of seats between the two parties in the House of Representatives will be fairly static over the course of the decade. If a district is 80 percent Democratic, it is not going be controlled by the Republicans even with a 10 or 20 percent vote swing toward the Republican Party.

However, it is very likely that in many states there will still be a chance to draw a district that is somewhat competitive. Imagine a state with ten seats in the House of Representatives and the partisanship of the state allows map makers to draw six districts packed with, on average, 90 percent Democrats, three districts with, on average, 90 percent Republican, and one district that is 55 percent Republican and 45 percent Democrats.[28] This last seat would be significantly more competitive in the general election than the other nine seats in the state. Thus, while the swing ratio will be close to zero using a packed partisan districting approach, it will not be zero and the distribution of seats in the House will respond to changes in voting patterns nationwide.

While there may be some wiggle room for some seats to be competitive, it is not clear to me that having an electoral system with a very low swing ratio is particularly problematic. This opinion, however, is not widely shared. Most people, be they scholars or members of the media, or even well-informed citizens, often decry how insulated the House of Representatives is already and believe that my approach would only make things worse. Those that disagree with me often find quotes from the founders on the subject of the role the House of Representatives would play in the federal government. The founders intended for the House of Representatives to be the institution that most closely mirrors the population at large. With more members and shorter terms than the Senate, the House would be the chamber of the legislature that would shift to the left or to the right as the voters shifted. Furthermore, originally Senators would be chosen not by the people but by the state legislatures of their respective states. Only the House was directly elected by the people themselves.

Consider this quote from John Adams:

> The principal difficulty lies, and the greatest care should be employed in constituting this Representative Assembly. It should be in miniature, an exact portrait of the people at large. It should think, feel, reason, and act like them. That it may be the interest of this Assembly to do strict justice at all times, it should be an equal representation or in other words equal interest among the people should have equal interest in it. Great care should be taken to effect this, and to prevent unfair, partial, and corrupt elections.[29]

Clearly Adams favors a close correspondence between the citizens and the legislature, but does this mean that he favors a highly responsive electoral system (i.e., one with a large swing ratio)? Not necessarily. If the House is a miniature version of the country then the distribution of seats between the two major parties ought to approximate the distribution of votes among the electorate. To mirror is to reflect with an accurate representation. To create an electoral system that exaggerates small changes in the voting behavior into relatively large seat swings is not necessarily the kind of reflection that we should be after. Indeed, one could easily think of a very highly responsive system as being a source of distortion in the translation of votes into seats, and not an accurate reflection. The fairest and most common-sense approach in translating votes into seats is to award seats in the legislature in proportion to the share of the votes that each party receives.

In some ways this type of redistricting scheme mimics a proportional representation electoral system with the two major parties being divided into districts to the extent that their voting base will allow. This system diverges from

PR in the sense that packing districts on the basis of party identification with the Democrats and Republicans will make it even more difficult for a third party candidate to win. One of the most common attributes of a PR system is that it facilitates the election of minor party candidates.[30] Thus, utilizing a fair partisan approach will make it even more difficult for a minor party candidate to win a seat in the House of Representatives, but the reality is that it is already virtually impossible for a third party candidate to win a seat in the House of Representatives. The cost then of reducing the odds of a minor party candidate winning an election from nearly zero to even nearer to zero is a small cost to pay given the benefits of switching to this districting method.

There is a tradeoff in a packed redistricting plan in which the swing ratio (or responsiveness of the system) is rather low; however, concomitant with that reduction, is the elimination of partisan bias in the map (as discussed in the previous chapter). Gerrymandering (which is what introduces partisan bias into a single-member district system) is a virtual impossibility if the two parties districts are packed at similar ratios (i.e., districts average 80 percent of one party or the other). The key is for there to exist some symmetry between the two parties with respect to the partisan strength that each party has in the districts that favor each party.[31] Thus, if the Republican districts average 75 percent Republican vote share, while the Democrat districts average just 60 percent Democratic vote share, then the plan is going to be biased toward the Democrats. Symmetry is a matching of partisan strength. So if there is an 80 percent Republican-leaning district, there should also be a district that is roughly 80 percent Democratic. While small or even moderate changes in the vote totals for the two parties will not translate into significant changes in their overall share of the seats in the House of Representatives, at the same time both parties will control a proportion of the seats that is roughly equal to the proportion of votes that their candidates command nationwide. There will be no underlying bias which can help one party, for instance, win a majority of the seats in a state despite the fact that they control less than a majority of the votes. Trading away some level of responsiveness is a small price to pay, in my mind, for the added benefit of a system with little to no partisan bias.

A related complaint is that a packed plan will "institutionalize" the majority party in the House of Representatives for an entire decade (until the lines can be redrawn again). This may very well be true, but the point is that this system translates a majority of the votes into a majority of the seats. Party identification in America is fairly stable, although voting tendencies are less so. So if the Democrats (Republicans) begin the decade as the majority party, the odds are that this party will also be the majority party at the end of the decade.

## Marginalization of Independents

Many American voters do not identify with either of the two major political parties in the country. In fact, it is well documented that since the middle of the twentieth century the number of voters who report that they consider themselves either a Democrat or a Republican has been steadily declining.[32] Voters have not become more negative toward the two parties, but rather, Wattenberg shows that voters are more neutral with respect to the Democrats and the Republicans. For instance, when asked to say anything either positive or negative about either the Democrats or Republicans, an increasing proportion of voters have nothing at all to say—nothing good or bad about either major political party in America.

If districts lines are drawn primarily on the basis of the underlying partisanship of the electorate, where does this leave Independent voters? First, it is important to quantify what proportion of the electorate that can truly be classified as Independent. Are we talking about 40 percent of the electorate or 4 percent? Fiorina criticized a packed districting plan with the following statistic: "this argument [in favor of packed districts] ignores the preferences of Independents (more than one-third of the population)."[33] Obviously, there is good reason to be suspicious of an electoral system that completely marginalizes over one-third of the voting electorate. Fortunately, the fair partisan approach described here does not ignore the preferences of a large proportion of the population. While this method clearly further institutionalizes the two major political parties, it is not the case, as I mentioned earlier, that Independent voters are having great success across the country electing Independent or third-party candidates at the moment either. Let me address several important issues that are highlighted by Fiorina's quote above.

First, the number of real Independents is far lower than the one-third of the population cited by Fiorina. We can use data from the American National Election Study survey series to get a reliable estimate. From the outset, it is important to note how political party identification questions are asked in the survey and the way in which respondents get coded as an Independent. Citizens are asked which party they identify themselves with and if they respond that they are an Independent, a follow-up question asks them if they feel closer to one of the two major political parties. In answering the follow-up question, if the respondent answers with "neither," then we classify her as a "pure Independent." However, if the interviewee feels closer to either the Democrats or Republicans, then she is classified as an Independent, but she "leans" toward one of the two major parties. For shorthand, we will refer to these voters as "Independent leaners," which indicates that these voters, while not explicitly identifying with one of the major American political parties, still feel closer to one of them rather than the other.

It turns out that these "leaners" act a lot like those respondents who are classified as straight partisans. Keith et al. demonstrate that Independents who "lean" toward one of the two major parties behave much like citizens who self-report as partisans.[34] So if someone says they are an Independent but see themselves as being closer to the Republican Party, they end up acting much more like someone who self-identifies as a Republican than so-called "pure"

Independents. Thus, the proper estimate for "Independents" is simply the number of pure Independents.

Figure 6.7 shows the percentage of the population from 1952–2000 that are Democrats, Republicans, and Independents. The proportion of Independents is both relatively low (it averages just over 10 percent for the entire time period) and fairly stable. So we are not talking about one voter in three, but more like one in ten. While ten percent of the voting public is a nontrivial amount, it is impossible for there to be no "wasted votes" in any single-member district system. The only time there are no votes for the losing candidate in a SMD system is when someone runs unopposed. Even when a strong incumbent faces a challenger that has no business even being on the ballot, the challenger inevitably receives many votes. Moreover, it is an explicit goal of a fair partisan districting plan to minimize the number of wasted votes, but lacking a move to proportional representation, it is impossible to not have some "wasted" votes.

Second, Fiorina misses the mark when he claims that independent voters will be overlooked or ignored. While this type of districting plan will not encourage the election of Independent or minor party candidates, the current constellation of district maps and the single-member district system itself reinforces the two-party system. The single-member district system, the Electoral College, and most electoral laws in the country all work against smaller or minor parties, keeping them from electing candidates to office. Only one

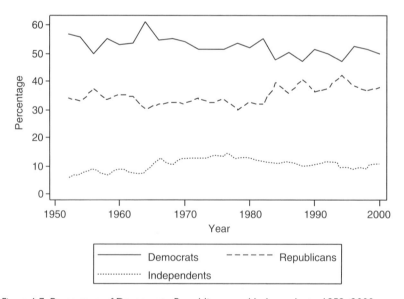

Figure 6.7 Percentage of Democrats, Republicans, and Independents, 1952–2000.

*Data from American National Election Study cumulative file 1952–2000. Party identification variable is vcf0301. Independents include only pure independents, and parties include identifiers and leaners.*

so-called Independent was in Congress in 2007—Bernie Sanders from Vermont. However, he caucuses with, and receives all of his committee assignments from the Democrats, so the degree of his independence is questionable. Independent voters are still able to participate in primary elections, which, again, would be the primary source of electoral choice and competition. Some states have enacted laws that restrict participating in a primary election to registered partisans—this type of election is referred to as a closed primary.[35] In these states, Independent voters would either have to get the state to change the rules or reregister with the dominant party in their district. Thus, even Independents can have an impact on who wins the primary (and then inevitably goes on to win the general election). Their participation in the electoral process would encourage (or even force) candidates for office to represent their independent interests in Congress.

## Losers would be more marginalized

Clearly the approach to redistricting that I am advocating here reduces the proportion of voters that see their preferred candidate lose the general election. Nonetheless, it is impossible in any single-member districting system to eliminate "losers" altogether. Indeed, given the distribution of partisans in a state, especially among Republicans, it may be difficult to draw a district with much more than 70 percent or so of one party in a district. Even if it is possible to draw a district with upwards of 90 percent of one party, that leaves 10 percent of the voters as "losers" and, perhaps worse still, these voters have no chance of electing their preferred candidate in the general election.

It is important to note that district lines do change every ten years, so the voters that may be part of the small losing proportion of voters in one decade are not necessarily going to be the same voters on the losing end after the following round of redistricting. If a Democratic voter lives in the middle of a very Republican area, they may very well end up on the losing end regardless of what the district lines look like just because of where they are situated. So it is likely that some small proportion of the voting public may be perennially on the losing side.

Do voters who have no chance whatsoever of choosing their candidate feel worse off than voters who at least have a perception that their vote may make a difference in the election? One could imagine that a voter in a district that leans nominally in favor of the other party may actually feel worse (less trust, satisfaction, and efficacy) than a voter who knows that his candidate of choice is not going to win from the outset. Expectations do matter and if someone expects that their candidate may have a chance, but the voter is still perpetually disappointed on Election Day, this may in fact make the voter worse off than a voter who simply has no expectation of winning given the composition of the district.

The proportion of losers among voters will be reduced and this fact ought to positively affect the overall disposition of voters with respect to their attitudes toward Congress. Moreover, as I showed in chapter 5, a packed districting plan has the effect of creating roughly proportional electoral outcomes at the state and national level. Anderson et al. show that losers in proportional systems are systematically more satisfied with democracy and have higher evaluations with respect to fairness and with respect to responsiveness of government.[36] A system that rewards parties with seats in the legislature that corresponds at least roughly with their share of the vote will be viewed as more fair relative to disproportionate outcomes. So even if a voter is dissatisfied because the specific district that he or she lives in may still be represented by a member from the "other" party, they may still be more satisfied with outcomes since the overall statewide (and nationwide) outcomes are proportional.

We tested the proposition that losers that lose by wider margins feel less efficacious or are less satisfied with their representative than losers whose candidate loses by a narrower margin in chapter 3. Recall that the critical component in determining satisfaction or efficacy is whether the voter's more preferred candidate wins the election, not the margin by which the candidate wins or loses.

## Conclusion

In this chapter I have addressed some of the most common and most serious claims about the possible negative effects of a packed redistricting plan. First, was the concern that drawing safe districts would tend to elect more radical members of Congress. It is not unfair to assume this, as at first blush it appears to make sense—if a Democrat has very few Republicans in the district to try to please, he will be pushed to the liberal end of the ideological spectrum. This assumption is, however, wrong. Just because a district is overwhelmingly Democratic, that does not mean that all the Democrats are all necessarily very liberal. If many of the voters tend to be moderate Democrats, which is a good naïve assumption, then the representative will tend toward the median moderate Democratic voters. I showed empirically that there is no relationship between the margin of victory that a member of the House wins by and the ideology of that member based on voting behavior on the floor of the House. So a Republican that wins 90 percent to 10 percent is not, on average, any more conservative than a Republican who is elected with just 51 percent of the vote. This should assuage the fears that Congress would function differently with the majority of seats in the House being safe compared to some alternative distribution of seats.

Next, I addressed the issue of whether creating overly safe seats in the House will encourage members to be less faithful to their voters. The answer is "no, it will not." Competition in the general election is not a necessary condition for keeping politicians interested in pleasing their constituents. Uneventful general elections do not remove electoral accountability from the equation. Moreover, there is scant evidence that shirking is a significant feature of the modern Congress and given that there are dozens of very safe members already, the notion that creating a Congress in which most members are "safe" in the general election will increase the incidence of shirking is clearly a nonstarter. As long as there is some degree of uncertainty about whether an incumbent will be reelected to office, he or she will be very interested in keeping the people happy. Since we have primary elections, forcing incumbents to effectively run the electoral gauntlet twice, no member regardless of how homogeneous the district, is truly "safe." Long-serving, entrenched members do manage to lose elections from time to time and these losses serve as notice to all incumbents that being complacent can cost them their job.

While I admit that the swing ratio or responsiveness of the electoral system for the House as a whole would decrease, with small changes in the voting behavior of Americans having little to no effect on the net distribution of seats between the two major parties, at the same time the added benefit of this is a sharp reduction in the amount of partisan bias in the system. The mapmakers hands are tied to such a degree that it is virtually impossible to draw a really effective partisan gerrymander since the districts will all be packed with either Democrats or Republicans.[37] The bottom line then is that the congressional delegation from each state will necessarily be closely reflective of the underlying partisan leanings of the voters in the state. It is not clear that having a very high swing ratio in an electoral system is, in and of itself, a good thing. Do we want electoral volatility? I am willing to take a low level of responsiveness in the system if there is no bias. It is important for the majority party in each state and in the country as a whole to win the most seats. It is also important for the two parties to be treated fairly and equally, which is to say that there should be no inherent partisan bias in the districting plan that robs one party of seats that they may otherwise win.

Next, I show that while Independent voters do make up 10 percent of the voting public (but certainly not over 30 percent as Fiorina suggests), there is no reason to expect that these people are disenfranchised. Since primary elections will be the focus of electoral competition in these districts, it is critical to participate in the primary and in many states (those with open primaries) anyone can participate in any party's primary election regardless of whether or not someone is registered partisan. In closed primary states, voters could reregister in the dominant party so that they too may participate in the primary election.

Last, I address the concern that the losing voters, who will inevitably exist in every district across the country, might be even more dissatisfied because there is virtually no chance whatsoever that their candidate can win the general election. First, district lines will change every ten years so there is not necessarily a sense of permanency to the district lines. Second, it is not clear that really marginalized losing voters will be less pleased than losers in districts with relatively close election outcomes since a voter's a priori expectations about the outcome will condition how they react to their candidate losing the election. This is to say if a voter fully expects to lose, she will not be particularly surprised when she does, whereas if she thinks her candidate can win and he never does, this could have an additional detrimental effect on attitudes toward government. Overall, while there are some costs associated with this type of districting plan, the benefits are legion and far outweigh the costs.

# Chapter 7

# Conclusion

Elections that provide real choices to voters remain critical in a democracy. Without choice the people have no way to provide real and direct inputs into the policy-making process. However, as I have argued throughout this book, we need not maximize the level of competitiveness in electoral districts across the country in order to satisfy this condition of electoral choice. In fact, since we use primary elections to choose among competing candidates in each party, the utility of competitive general elections is quite low. Instead of drawing competitive districts that simply maximize the number of losing voters, and can lead to incredibly disproportionate outcomes in the aggregate, we ought to do the opposite, which is to draw highly uncompetitive, ideologically homogeneous districts. I understand that this is a provocative argument, but I want to ensure the reader than I am not making this argument simply to provoke; I do believe that the views of American voters would be better represented and voters would be more satisfied with that representation if we changed our approach to redistricting.

## Reforming redistricting?

It seems like redistricting reform is always on someone's agenda somewhere in the country. The general sense that one gets is that most people are dissatisfied with the process of redistricting, as well as with the outcomes. By having elected state legislators draw their own district lines and the district lines for the state delegation to the House of Representatives, the process feels unseemly. The popular view of the current methods of redistricting in America is generally fairly negative. Indeed, it is hard to find anything but scorn and accusations in any article that addresses this critical issue. The following is typical:

> Redistricting in America is rotten. Across the country, for elections of every level, district lines are drawn in such a way that fundamental democratic values are subverted. Sometimes districts take on bizarre shapes as legislators add and subtract people in order to assure a particular political profile. Sometimes distinct political communities—say, rural farmers or

inner-city minorities—are split apart by district lines or merged with other very different communities. Sometimes districts are blatantly skewed toward one party even though the state as a whole is political competitive. Sometimes, thanks to clever district-drawing, the distribution of seats in a state legislature or congressional delegation has little correlation to a state's overall voting pattern. And, very often, all these sins are combined. When looking at a district map, it is not unusual to see an oddly shaped district that divided political communities, virtually guaranteed reelection for incumbents, and enabled one party to win a much higher proportion of legislative seats than popular votes."[1]

While no one would ever accuse elected officials of being generous or angelic during the redistricting process, the hyperbole above is all too common. Are some districts oddly shaped? Of course, districts often need to be drawn in odd shapes in order to comply with the Voting Rights Act and the *Gingles* decision. Congressional districts are often drawn in such a manner that one party is advantaged in nearly all districts even if the elections are competitive statewide. But just because a state is at near partisan parity does that mean that every district, or even some of the districts, have to be competitive? Of course not. Are there really gerrymanders so effective that the distribution of seats in the state legislature or congressional delegation has virtually no correlation with the state's overall voting pattern? No, this is the classic overstatement that somehow the lines are so tortured that a party with no votes statewide somehow manages a majority in the state legislature or the congressional delegation. Have parties that are marginally in the minority managed to control a majority of the state legislature or the congressional delegation? Yes, as was seen in Texas most recently in the 1990s, but this does not happen in most states. In order to be in control of drawing new districts, a party has to have a majority of the seats in the state legislature and control the governor-ship. In order to have majorities in the chambers of the state legislature and to control the governorship, a party needs votes. In fact, a party needs most of the votes statewide, and without these votes they cannot control the redistricting process and therefore they cannot gerrymander a map.

Redistricting draws rampant criticisms though because the politicians are in control, they are self-interested, and there is undoubtedly some creative line drawing involved. However, most redistricting efforts do not constitute a gerrymander. Redistricting is not subverting fundamental democratic values and the sky is not falling. Clearly, I do agree that there ought to be some reforms to the approach of redistricting, but my recommendations are not of the usual variety. The article quoted earlier argues in favor of nonpartisan redistricting commissions, which are not a cure-all to the problem to be sure.

Reforming the process by which we redistrict is often pursued by a variety of groups in every state throughout the country. Taking the power to redistrict away from state legislators appeals to most folks at a very basic level as it makes sense to take power away from people who have a critical stake in the outcome. Some citizens and virtually every pundit seems to feel that if we can just get the politicians out of the redistricting process and hand it over to judges, or experts, or nonpartisan commissions, or anybody but another elected official, then things would be better. This is not, in my opinion, the best route to take. Reforming the process, regardless of what the reform looks like, does not take the politics out of redistricting. Some would say "you can't take the politics out of redistricting, but you can take the politicians out of redistricting," but I do not see how this solves any problems.

Let us assume that a state is thinking about passing a law to create a "nonpartisan independent redistricting commission" and removing the state legislature from the process altogether. Numerous states have recently been considering these types of bills including California, Florida, and Ohio. And many other states have tried to reform the redistricting process in this manner by passing popular initiatives. Indeed, there have been at least 12 different reform-minded initiatives aimed at the redistricting process over the years in several different states. Stephanopoulous documents these various attempts going all the way back to a 1936 ballot proposal in Arkansas that passed.[2] The voters in California have had no fewer than four separate opportunities to institute reforms via the initiative process, but every single one of them was voted down.

The first problem with reforms of this ilk (i.e., giving the power to an independent commission) is that the bodies created to draw new electoral lines are neither "nonpartisan" nor "independent." Commissions have to be run by someone, and everyone has a political position. There must be a method for selecting the members of the commission, which is typically done by allowing various elected state officials to pick a member, or by letting the Democrats pick half the members, and then letting the Republicans pick the other half. In that sense a much better adjective is "bipartisan" insofar as it is somewhat descriptive, but a better descriptor might be "deadlocked." When we create an institution that is staffed by equal numbers of Democrats and Republicans, and hand them a political task, we cannot be surprised when this group is unable to make a decision. In all likelihood when it comes time to vote, the Democrats will all support one plan and the Republicans another. Because the commission is built to deadlock there must be a method for breaking a tie, when the inevitable happens. Clearly the provision to break a tie on these commissions is going to be critical (i.e., decisive). How is this person picked? Should the Chief Justice of the State Supreme Court do it? Should we pick a name out of a hat? Suffice it to say that regardless of who gets picked and how they get picked, there are going to be people bent out of shape at the end of the day because they got the short end of the stick.

In New Jersey they utilize a ten-member apportionment commission—comprised of five Democrats and five Republicans to redraw the state legislative district lines every ten years. Naturally, every time the commission has gone to work for the last three rounds of redistricting (1980s, 1990s, and 2000s), the commission could not come to an agreement. When this happens (i.e., every time the commission is formed), the Chief Justice of the New Jersey State Supreme Court is tasked with appointing a nonpartisan eleventh member of the commission to break the tie. For the last three decades this critical position was filled by a political science professor from Princeton.[3] The critical vote then is left to a college professor, and while there are surely worse people to break a logjam than a political scientist, I think these tasks are better left to elected officials and not unresponsive appointees.[4]

The more general problem of how to populate a commission once it has been created is quite tricky. Why are appointed members better than elected members? I think the underlying logic would go something like this: appointees have no electoral incentive themselves and therefore they will not bias the map in favor of themselves. But it is because they have no electoral incentive at all that they are free to do whatever they want. They have been authorized to do a job and face no penalty or repercussions if the state does not like what they have done.

If we decide to use appointed boards to draw electoral boundaries, the next question is how do we appoint these people? Should party leaders get an equal number of seats to fill on the commission? Should we designate specific state posts that get to appoint one or more members? Who is eligible to serve on the commission? Should it be nonpartisan? How do we know when someone is a Republican or Democrat? Usually it is by how they have registered to vote. Party registration is trivial to change and is a particularly good predictor of how the person will act. What kind of experience with districting should they have, if any? Should we restrict the population of possible members to retired judges in the state? There are a myriad of problems and questions that must be addressed.

My approach to the commission problem is to undertake a simple thought experiment—if you were going to design the best group of people to draw the district lines, what would you devise? In my mind, elections are uniformly better at selecting people than appointments, so let the people decide who is going to sit on the board. Next, we need to make sure that people across the state are equally represented on the redistricting board, so we can carve the state up into several districts with roughly equal population in all the districts and elect one person from each district. While this solution is not perfect, it seems to be a reasonably fair approach—we need not worry about who to appoint and how to appoint people to a commission, and interests across the state will be represented. This simple "solution," if it is not clear already, has done nothing more than recreate the state legislature. State legislators are, in my mind, the best people to tackle the tough task of redistricting. The task is not an easy one to accomplish, and redistricting is never done without some feathers being ruffled and someone's ox being gored, nonetheless these people are elected to handle the important problems facing the state, and clearly drawing electoral districts falls into this category.

Process-oriented solutions to the redistricting problem are rarely effective. Someone needs to draw a new map and regardless of who the people are or how they are chosen, politics plays a role in the process and the outcome. In that case, we ought to keep the process in the hands of elected officials— politicians who can be removed from office if they do something to displease the voters. Unelected commissioners are not incentivized to be responsive and so they do not have to worry what the people think. In order to successfully change the outcomes from redistricting, we do not need to change who manages the process, but rather on what principles the map makers must be constrained.

Adam Cox has some interesting ideas in terms of reforms that move beyond taking the power away from the state legislatures. Cox suggests that the power remain with the elected state legislators, but that there be temporal veil rules put in place that somewhat constrain the ability of map makers to create a gerrymandered electoral plan.[5] In short, Cox argues that state legislators must draw a map behind a "partial veil of ignorance" so that there is more uncertainty with respect to the political effects of any given set of district lines. One form of the "temporal veil" suggested by Cox is to delay implementation of the new map, so that a map is drawn in one year, but not implemented in the very next electoral cycle, but rather later on in the decade. This would decrease the certainty with which safe districts could be drawn. A district might look like a 60 percent Democratic district today, but what will it look like five years from now? To some extent this already happens insofar as districts are typically left intact for the entire decade.[6]

Other possible avenues of reform include restricting the type of data that redistricters are permitted to use. Typically when drawing a map, the analyst wants to have as much data at the lowest level of aggregation as possible. Some of the typical political data used to get an idea about which way the district will lean politically include party registration data (i.e., how do precincts break down in terms of party registration) and also election data at the precinct level. One does need to pick which election or combination of elections to use for this task, and typically the analyst tries to pick a recent statewide or presidential election between two good candidates that did not end in a landslide. These two kinds of data really can do a good job of predicting the partisan predilections of a would-be district. So instead of allowing the technicians to use all different kinds of election data and party registration data merged with geographic data, we force them to use just census data. This would then focus the map makers on creating compact, equally populous districts, and, to the extent that they need to comply with the Voting Rights Act, racially based redistricting enters the picture. Here, the idea is that by robbing the map makers of the data that allows them to fine tune districts with respect to the underlying partisan nature of the districts, the set of districts they create would somehow be more pure. While having data on party registration or voting data at very low levels of aggregation undoubtedly makes creating a gerrymandered map easier, these data have not always been as readily accessible as they are today and the gerrymander is significantly older than the advent of modern computing. This avenue of reform is not that appealing since there are people with sufficient "local" knowledge about the politics relating to geography that this brand of reform is destined to fail.

Another interesting possibility for redistricting in the future is fully automated computerized or algorithmic map making. Here one programs a computer to fulfill certain parameters, such as to minimize population deviations from ideal and draw districts composed of only contiguous whole counties. Obviously the criterion by which the computer begins cutting up the state is critical—different parameters will yield different results. Hayes does some interesting experimentation with different sorts of algorithms to carve up the state of North Carolina.[7] Naturally he gets different results depending on the algorithm, but overall the methods have a component of randomness, which would create a great deal of uncertainty in the minds of elected officials with respect to what their district might look like post-redistricting. At some level it might seem unfair to members of Congress or state legislatures to have them grow accustom to a certain district, in the sense that they probably provide better representation for the district the longer they represent the same area, and then pull the rug out from beneath them by chopping up the district in such a way that the new district looks nothing like the old one. Nonetheless, this kind of reform is appealing to some people simply because it is automated and feels more objective, but that does not mean that it is not without significant problems of its own. As Hayes puts it

> The algorithmic approach offers an alternative, but it would require a major shift in attitude and expectations—a meta-political revolution. No longer would redistricting be an opportunity to seize political advantage; it would have to be seen as a neutral or arbitrary event, beyond human control, above politics, subject to luck, much like the random choice of which candidate's name is listed first on a ballot. Redistricting would also be lost as an instrument for achieving social goals, such as creating a more racially balanced Congress.[8]

Hayes is spot on with his assessment here insofar as everyone would have to agree to give up the chance at gaining some political advantage by accepting that there is some serious random component to what the constellation of new districts will look like. From the perspective of the elected official, nothing could be worse. This kind of randomness tends to strike terror in the hearts of legislators because anyone could become a victim of the new map. I suspect that even legislators who are in a state's minority party, and therefore subject to a gerrymander on the part of the opposition, would prefer not to have a random component because the other side can only do so much harm to the minority party with creative map making, whereas the randomness would just keep everyone up at night, worried about what might happen.

Reforming the process of redistricting is not particularly useful. Trying to leech politics out of an inherently partisan process is a lot like squeezing blood from a turnip. Effecting better, more representative electoral districts has to be done by setting the parameters by which districts are drawn. At the moment, the restrictions do not really tie the hands of would-be gerrymanderers. So districts have to be equally populous and contiguous, that does not really hamstring self-interested people from being creative with the boundaries. Some states have to worry about majority–minority districts, but even these districts can work to the advantage of one party or the other. Limiting the kinds of political data available to map makers seems like it would not be particularly effective. Rather if we set much stricter guidelines, then it is possible to really have an impact on what these maps look like. My proposal is to draw districts to maximize the proportion of either Democrats or Republicans in each district, with some artificial percentage as a goal for each district. So a state sets out to make each district comprised of 80 percent of either Democrats or Republicans. Districts may not end up looking particularly pretty, but, as I argued earlier, the shape of a district is not all that important. Rather than maximizing the importance of ideology and minimizing the importance of geography, most people prefer to do the opposite (by creating competitive districts) and try to severely limit what can be done in the process by setting stringent guidelines with respect to protecting political sub-divisions such as county or municipal lines, or by increasing the importance of compactness in districts.

## Do we really need more electoral competition?

We have all been sold a bill of goods about the inherent necessity of electoral competition to a smoothly functioning democracy. Political scientists have grown so accustomed to directly linking the responsiveness of representatives to electoral competition that we do not really stop to think if this causal connection is real. This connection has become so much of the "common wisdom" that no one even considers the possibility that there are many other forces at work (e.g., the presence of primary elections, or the real degree of uncertainty necessary to keep members responsive) that encourage members to represent their district as best they can and that general election competitiveness is not really all that important. It is time for us to think more carefully about this, as the connection is clearly more tenuous than the common wisdom has lead us to believe.

Here are some excerpts from an opinion piece that appeared in the *Washington Post* in 2001:

- "We draw new lines deliberately designed to keep the incumbents from losing. Those lines are a noose around democracy."
- "It's not gerrymandering in favor of Republicans or Democrats; the mischief is bipartisan. It makes one district safe for one party and the adjoining district safe for another. The truth is that both parties want it that way."
- "So when it's time to redistrict, the people doing it simply draw a line like a lasso and rope the Democrats out of the Republican district next door, which of course makes that district even more Republican, and vice versa."
- "The result is that the incumbent cannot be defeated, and the voters in effect are disenfranchised."
- "Unlosable districts are a far greater threat to the voter than butterfly ballots."[9]

Collectively, these quotes do a very good job summarizing the long-held beliefs about the ills of redistricting and the need for competition in American elections. Fortunately for us, all of these quotes are, in part or in whole, wrong. If districts were really unlosable, then this would indeed be a threat to democracy. But it is impossible to draw a district that is unlosable. It may be virtually impossible to beat the incumbent in the general election, but no elected official is safe in the primary election stage. I am not the only one to recognize this; for instance, the following is from the editorial pages of an American newspaper: "Voters have two shots: the primary and the general election. The lines can be drawn so that favored incumbents are protected in the general election. But not in the primary."[10] There is no noose around democracy, in fact the result so often decried as political sabotage is in fact improving representation and democracy in America. Competitive elections are not the solution; they are part of the problem.

Competitive general elections for the U.S. House of Representative and state legislatures across the country are not vital for good representation or responsive representation. Indeed, competitive elections increase the number of people who do not care for the outcome of the election and are left unrepresented in Congress. Congressional and legislative elections are similar insofar as it is possible to artificially manufacture competition since the electoral district boundaries are fluid. Obviously when we are talking about presidential, senatorial, or gubernatorial elections, then either the elections are competitive or they are not—there is nothing that we can do about it since the district lines for these offices never change, but for those offices that do undergo redistricting we need to rethink our approach. Even more problematic in terms of redistricting is that drawing competitive districts does *not* mean that there will in fact be a competitive election in that district. Competitive districts are neither a necessary nor sufficient condition for competitive elections. Naturally, the two are correlated, which is to say that districts drawn with rough parity between the two parties are more likely to have a competitive general election relative to districts drawn otherwise, but there is no guarantee that whomever gets elected cannot consolidate power in the district to such a degree that potential high-quality challengers choose not to run against the incumbent. In political science this is known as the "sophomore surge," which describes the tendency of incumbents running for their second term, on average, to do much better in the second election relative to the first time they were elected.

The fact that most people have a knee-jerk reaction about the need for more competition in congressional elections is not surprising. First, there are many good reasons to think that competitiveness is crucial to a properly functioning democracy. Voters should have a real choice when they cast their ballot. Representatives should not be so well insulated in office that they have virtually no chance of being replaced in an election. Deliberation among voters and between candidates about what course the country should follow is beneficial to both voters and elected officials. Competitiveness is ingrained in the American culture. Americans compete on so many different levels and in so many different venues, that more competition always seems like a good idea. In the case of general elections for the House of Representatives and state legislative elections, we do need more competition, but where we need this competitiveness is at the primary election stage.

Rather than increasing competitiveness by drawing districts with near parity in terms of the party identification (or voting patterns) among the electorate, we need to minimize ideological diversity, which will also minimize general election competitiveness, as much as possible. Diverse districts are not easily represented and by purposefully crafting districts to increase diversity, we force many voters to be unhappy with their representation in the House. What is a liberal in Tom Delay's district to do? What about a conservative stuck living in Nancy Pelosi's district? Diversity, a necessary component for competitiveness, is the enemy of accurate and solid representation. The more diverse the opinions of the voters in the district, the less well any single representative can translate the preferences of the constituency into behavior on Capitol Hill.

People prefer to win. This is true when we are talking about someone's favorite football team. or someone's Thursday night poker game. More importantly, it is also true when we are talking about elections. Voters take sides and they, naturally, want their side, their preferred candidates, to win. If this were not true, it is unlikely that anyone would vote at all. When someone does vote for the winning candidate they are far more satisfied with their representation compared to those voters who cast a ballot for the candidate that lost the election. This statement is true irrespective of how one imagines voters making decisions. Do voters choose their candidate based on party identification or on ideological proximity or retrospective evaluations of the economy? It does not matter. What matters is that they have picked a side and are going to be more satisfied when their candidate actually wins the election and takes office.

For those elections that do use artificial boundaries we can maximize the number of winners by increasing the ideological homogeneity within districts. Optimally, we would draw voters into districts in which the ideological variance was quite low, so perhaps we would have a "socially liberal but fiscally conservative district" in Illinois, or a "pro-gun, pro-life Democratic" district in Pennsylvania. Tailor making districts like this would not be easy and in most cases it might be impossible. The geographic link really restricts the kinds of districts that are possible in a system of representation, whereas a nationwide party list proportional representation system would naturally group people in several parties with strong ideological incentives more so than in the single-member district system currently in place. However, working within the confines of the single-member district system, we could get along quite far just by grouping Democrats with Democrats and Republicans with Republicans in electoral districts. To be sure, there are many shades of ideology within each of these large political parties, but it is possible to draw districts in such a way that it would significantly reduce the amount of ideological diversity within the districts.

A good way to summarize the packed district plan presented here is a system of proportional representation (PR) crammed into a single-member district electoral system. We could, of course, simply adopt a system of proportional representation and save ourselves a significant amount of trouble. While this is true, it is highly unlikely to happen any time soon, and it would require major changes in federal law and perhaps even some changes to the Constitution itself. The plan presented here requires no such changes to any federal law and can be implemented at any time, we just need to change the way in which we think about redistricting, and thus, how we draw district lines. But while this plan may theoretically be feasible within the current structure of federal law, another important question is whether or not it really is feasible to draw districts in this manner.

While I have never drawn an electoral district map in my life, I have been involved with redistricting for some time and I consulted with several people who have drawn dozens and even hundreds of districting maps over the last two or three cycles of redistricting. The general consensus was "yes it can be done, but it will not work the same way in every state or for every office." From my discussion throughout this book it should be obvious that the more packed a district, the better. Which is to say if all districts in a state can be drawn 90–10, that is better than all the districts being drawn with an 80–20 split. While districts that are 90–10 are almost certainly unachievable, and 80–20 might be quite difficult to do in every state, something along these lines is well within the realm of the possible. The question is not whether the packed partisan plan is feasible, but just the degree to which it is feasible in each state.

One of Lani Guinier's most powerful criticisms about the single member district system is that the redistricting process will inherently result in a gerrymander because "in essence redistricting is the process of distributing wasted votes" (Guinier 1993). Guinier's fears are rather well founded given the traditional districting process, however much of her concerns generally about single-member districts and the redrawing of their lines disappear using the method outlined in this book.

For instance, Guinier writes specifically about the kind of redistricting that I have in mind (i.e., creating homogeneous districts):

> "Districts could be made more homogeneous to reduce the number of wasted votes. But this alternative demonstrates the second way that winner-take-all districting waste votes. When more people vote for the winning candidate than is necessary to carry the district, their votes are technically wasted because they were unnecessary to provide an electoral margin within the district and they could have been used to provide the necessary electoral margin for a like-minded partisan in another district. In other words, packing voters in homogeneous districts wastes votes because it dilutes their overall voting strength jurisdiction-wide.

This is an important point insofar as a gerrymander is only possible when one uses the combined strategy of packing and cracking. However, if all districts are packed then the real problem Guinier addresses above is solved. Votes in packed districts are not effectively wasted because all districts are packed, and the overvotes could not be used to help a like-minded partisan in another district. While there are always some overvotes that are wasted, we explicitly try to minimize these kinds of votes.

The first issue is how do we count people as either Democrat or Republican? Do we use party registration? The problem with registration data is that some states do not have registration by party, and in the states that do have party registration there are many people who register with a third party, or as an Independent, or as "decline to state." These voters usually make up a significant portion of the population. This means the basis for drawing districts would have to be election results. One possibility is to use the last presidential election broken up by the smallest geographic unit possible in the state. Another one uses an important statewide race, such as the gubernatorial election or a senatorial election, as the key partisan data. Perhaps we average over several elections. There is not a single answer to this question, but it is certainly not an intractable problem.

The real difficultly lies in trying to split up ideological diverse precincts. Inner-city districts with very high densities of minorities are perfect for this kind of districting plan because of the lack of partisan diversity. As one moves to the suburbs, things become more difficult. As the building blocks of districting maps, voting precincts, become more diverse, it becomes increasingly difficult to draw homogeneous districts. In general, as geographical diversity of ideology increases, the more difficult it will be to draw packed districts. While higher proportions of like-minded partisans is always better from my perspective, if geography only allows drawing 70–30 or even 60–40 districts, the end result is still worth the effort. The key is to maximize the number of winners, while also drawing each major party's districts to the same proportion, which eliminates bias (i.e., gerrymanders).

The question of the feasibility of a packed partisan plan is an important one. The good news, as I mentioned earlier, is that it can be done; the only question is the degree to which it can be done. The goal is to set a target number, maybe it is 70 or 75 or even 80, and try to make each district as close to that target as possible with either Democrats or Republicans. As long as districts for both sides average out to roughly the same number, then the overall fairness of the plan is assured. So what should be done if in one state it is not possible to draw Republican districts that average 70, but it is possible to draw Democratic districts that average 70? The target number must be lowered. Both sides have to be treated equally so the districts have to be diluted so that the averages are nearly identical. Perhaps the target in this state must be 68, since this is the highest value that can be achieved for *both parties*. So again, implementing this plan does not hinge on some special set of circumstances, but rather the distribution of votes across a state will determine the degree to which districts can be packed. A higher target number is always better, but in some states enacting a map with heavily packed districts is going to be more difficult.

Some people have mentioned that the approach put forth in this book is already in effect in many states. Scholars and pundits have begun complaining about what has become known as a "bipartisan gerrymander." In short, this phrase refers to a plan that basically keeps all the current incumbents, from both parties, relatively safe (in the general election). This is to say, the map makers have not gone out of their way to draw competitive districts. Of course most people are not particularly happy with the so-called bipartisan gerrymander because of the misplaced commitments we have for competitiveness in the general election. As an example—Fiorina writes: "In a partisan gerrymander, one party attempts to screw the other. In a bipartisan gerrymander both parties agree on a plan to divvy up the seats."[11] At times this approach is also called an "incumbent protection gerrymander." I am not fond of using the word gerrymander in either of these phrases. It uses the word too loosely. A gerrymander is a redistricting plan that is asymmetrical with respect to the way in which votes are translated into seats for the political parties. For instance, a plan can pack and crack Republicans so that when they get 50 percent of the vote statewide, they only get 45 percent of the seats. This, of course, means that the Democrats received 55 percent of the seats with the same percentage of the vote (50 percent). The dictionary defines a gerrymander as "To divide (a geographic area) into voting districts so as to give unfair advantage to one party in elections."[12] Thus, a gerrymander is inherently partisan, so there can be no such thing as a bipartisan gerrymander—the phrase is an oxymoron. I suspect one of the reasons the phrase emerged is because the word gerrymander is a pejorative and attaching this word to a map that treats both parties fairly, but lacks electoral competition, encourages other people to disapprove of this approach. We should strike the phrase bipartisan gerrymander or incumbent protection gerrymander from the lexicon and replace it with a more appropriate phrase, perhaps "fair bipartisan plan" or "packed partisan plan."

Everyone has heard some rendition of the following phrase: "You can please some of the people all of the time, all of the people some of the time, but you cannot please all of the people all of the time." This statement is true in a general sense and in a specific sense as applied to redistricting. You cannot please all of the people all of the time, but we can stop trying to please as few people as possible by drawing competitive district and instead try to maximize the number of people we please by drawing districts packed with like-minded partisans. By doing so, the proportion of voters who vote for the winner will increase, as will the proportion of voters who are satisfied with their particular member of Congress and Congress as an institution. It is virtually impossible to gerrymander if districts are drawn in this manner and this system mimics a proportional representation system insofar as the overall proportion of seats held by the major parties in a state legislature or in a congressional delegation will closely match the underlying partisanship of the state. The sooner we stop the collective hand-wringing about the lack of competition in House elections, the better. Noncompetitive districts make for better representatives and better representation.

# Notes

## I Introduction

1 *Talk of the Nation*, Friday November 5, 2004.
2 "Blue state blues cure in Canada?" by George Lewis, NBC correspondent, MSNBC.com. Retrieved on 12/15/2005 from www.msnbc.msn.com/id/6694546/.
3 See Morris Fiorina. 2006. *Culture War? The Myth of a Polarized America*. 2nd edition. New York: Pearson Longman.
4 See Michael Barone, "The 49 Percent Nation," *National Journal*, June 8, 2001.
5 In the early years of the Republic, states did not actually lose seats in this process as the House of Representatives would just increase the number of seats in the body to accommodate more states and the growing population of other states. It was not until the size of the House was fixed in 1920 that reapportionment became a zero sum game.
6 Moreover, it is not clear what makes one map of electoral districts "better" than another. Some people want to maximize the number of competitive districts, while others prefer to keep as many cities and counties whole inside electoral districts.
7 "The Great Election Grab," by Jeffrey Toobin in *The New Yorker*, 12/8/2003.
8 "Governor says redistricting needed; Democrat calls plan power grab," by Steve Lawrence, *San Francisco Chronicle*, 2/24/2005.
9 Sam Hirsch. 2003. "The United States House of Unrepresentatives: What Went Wrong in the Latest Round of Congressional Redistricting." *Election Law Journal* 2(2): 179–216.
10 Thomas E. Mann and Bruce E. Cain. 2005. "Introduction" in *Party Lines*, Thomas E. Mann and Bruce E. Cain (eds). Washington DC: Brooking Press, p. 1.
11 "Redistricting Dance," *The Times Union*, November 16, 2005.
12 Clearly the partisan makeup of a district affects the likelihood of a high-quality challenger emerging, as do many other variables.
13 www.fairvote.org/?page=111 (accessed 2/1/2006).
14 Cox, Gary W. and Jonathan N. Katz. 2002. *Elbridge Gerry's Salamander: The Electoral Consequences of the Reapportionment Revolution*. Cambridge: Cambridge University Press.
15 This was a quote from Don Perata, the Democratic leader of the California state Senate, who headed the redistricting effort for the Senate in 2001.
16 Hannah F. Pitkin. 1967. *The Concept of Representation*. Berkeley: University of California Press.

17 There is a saying that the biggest lie in Washington is that someone is leaving office "to spend more time with the family." Much more likely they are about to be defeated in the next election. Cox and Katz (2002) call this dynamic "strategic exit." An incumbent facing a high probability of defeat will retire "voluntarily" and this affects our estimates of the incumbency advantage because these elections in which the incumbent loses never happen.

18 Malcolm E. Jewell and Lee Sigelman. 1986. "Voting in Primaries: The Impact of Intra- and Inter-Party Competition." *The Western Political Quarterly.* 39(3): 446–454.

19 John R. Hibbing and Elizabeth Theiss-Morse. 1995. *Congress as Public Enemy: Public Attitudes towards American Political Institutions.* Cambridge: Cambridge University Press.

20 This is not to say that this approach will lend itself to districts that are not oddly shaped as it will, but remember that noncompact districts are neither a necessary nor sufficient condition for a plan that constitutes a gerrymander. We are not so much worried about the shape or underlying beauty of the districts, but rather how votes get translated into seats.

21 Warren E. Miller and Donald E. Stokes. 1963. "Constituency Influence in Congress." *American Political Science Review* 57(1): 45–56. Quote on page 56.

## 2 Theories of representation

1 Bernard Manin. 1997. *The Principles of Representative Government.* Cambridge: Cambridge University Press.

2 Robert A. Dahl. 1956. *A Preface to Democratic Theory.* Chicago: University of Chicago Press, page 95.

3 Dahl "Preface," page 95.

4 Hannah F. Pitkin. 1967. *The Concept of Representation.* Berkeley: University of California Press, page 55.

5 Pitkin "Representation," page 55.

6 Ibid., page 61.

7 Ibid., page 61.

8 Ibid., page 89.

9 Ibid., page 92.

10 Eulau, Heinz and Paul D. Karps. 1977. "The Puzzle of Representation: Specifying Components of Responsiveness." *Legislative Studies Quarterly* 2(3): 233–254. Quote on page 241.

11 Verba, Sidney and Norman H. Nie. 1972. *Participation in America: Political Democracy and Social Equality.* New York: Harper and Row.

12 Eulau and Karps, page 246.

13 Andrew Rehfeld. 2005. *The Concept of Constituency: Political Representation, Democratic Legitimacy and Institutional Design.* Cambridge: Cambridge University Press.

14 Fiorina, Morris P. 1974. *Representatives, Roll Calls, and Constituencies.* Lexington MA: Lexington Books.

15 Huntington, Samuel. 1950. "A Revised Theory of American Party Parties." *American Political Science Review* 44(3):669–677.

16 Schumpeter, Joseph. 1942. *Capitalism, Socialism, and Democracy.* New York: Harper and Row.

17 Ibid., page 262.

18 Ibid., page 262.

19  Ibid., page 269.
20  Ibid., page 272.
21  McCrone, Donald J. and James H. Kuklinski. 1979. "The Delegate Theory of Representation." *American Journal of Political Science* 23(2): 278–300.
22  Downs, Anthony. 1957. *An Economic Theory of Democracy*. New York: Harper and Row.
23  The median minimizes the value of sum of absolute deviations, while the mean minimizes the sum of squared deviations in a distribution. In the normal distribution the mean and the median are coincidental.
24  Fenno, Richard F. 1978. *Home Style: House Members in Their Districts*. Boston: Little, Brown.

## 3  Voters prefer to win elections

1  Anderson, Christopher J. and Andrew J. LoTempio. 2002. "Winning, Losing and Political Trust in America." *British Journal of Political Science* 32: 335–351.
2  They tested both voting for the winning candidate in an election and voting for the party that wins a majority in Congress; neither model yielded statistically significant results.
3  Clarke, Harold D., and Alan C. Acock. 1989. "National Elections and Political Attitudes: The Case of Political Efficacy." *British Journal of Political Science* 19(4): 551–562.
4  Clarke and Acock do not find evidence of this pure outcome effect at the congressional level, which they ascribe largely to the effects of knowledge— virtually everyone (including nonvoters) knows who wins the presidential election. Congressional election outcomes do not have this level of salience.
5  Brunell, Thomas L. and Justin Buchler. 2007. "Ideological Representation and Competitive Congressional Districts: Some Empirical Observations." Typescript, University of Texas at Dallas.
6  Brunell, Thomas L. 2006. "Rethinking Redistricting: How Drawing Uncompetitive Districts Eliminates Gerrymanders, Enhances Representation, and Improves Attitudes Toward Congress." *PS: Political Science and Politics* 39(1) 77–86.
7  Barreto, Matt. and Streb, Matthew. 2007. "Barn Burners and Burn Out: The Effects of Competitive Elections on Efficacy and Trust." Paper presented at the annual meeting of the Midwest Political Science Association.
8  Anderson, Christopher J., and Christine A. Guillory. 1997. "Political Institutions and Satisfaction with Democracy: A Cross-National Analysis of Consensus and Majoritarian Systems." *American Political Science Review* 91(1): 66–81.
9  Clarke, Harold D., and Allan Kornberg. 1992. "Do National Elections Affect Perceptions of MP Responsiveness? A Note on the Canadian Case." *Legislative Studies Quarterly* 17(2): 183–204.
10  Bowler, Shaun and Todd Donovan. 2002. "Democracy, Institutions and Attitudes about Citizen Influence on Government." *British Journal of Political Science* 32(4): 371–390.
11  Anderson Christopher J., André Blais, Shaun Bowler, Todd Donovan, and Ola Listhaug. 2005. *Losers' Consent: Elections and Democratic Legitimacy*. Oxford: Oxford University Press, page 3.
12  Ibid., page 3.
13  Ibid., page 186.

14  Regan, Dennis T. and Martin Kilduff. 1988. "Optimism about elections: dissonance reduction at the ballot box." *Political Psychology* 9(1): 101–107.

15  Ibid., page 106.

16  Granberg, Donald and Edward Brent. 1983. "When Prophecy Bends: The Preference-expectation Link in U.S. Presidential Elections, 1952–1980. *Journal of Personality and Social Psychology* 45: 477–491.

17  See William Koetzle. 1998. "The Impact of Constituency Diversity upon the Competitiveness of U.S. House of Representatives Elections, 1962–1996." *Legislative Studies Quarterly* 23: 561–574

18  Typically, when political scientists talk about the "quality" of a candidate we mean that if a candidate has held elective office before, the candidate is a high-quality candidate and if the candidate has never held any prior elective office, they are a low-quality candidate.

19  Anderson et al. *Loser's Consent.*

20  Koetzle 1998.

21  Anderson and LoTempio "Winning, Losing, and Political Trust."

22  This is tempered by the fact that American voters cast ballots in numerous elections every time they go to the polls, including several (president, senator, and governor) that are probably more important in voters' minds than the House election.

23  See John R. Hibbing and Elizabeth Theiss-Morse. 1995. *Congress as Public Enemy: Public Attitudes towards American Political Institutions.* Cambridge: Cambridge University Press. As well as John R. Hibbing and James T. Smith. 2001. "What the American Public Wants Congress to Be," in *Congress Reconsidered.* 7th edition. Eds Lawrence C. Dodd and Bruce I. Oppenheimer. Washington DC: CQ Press.

24  Cracking refers to the art of drawing districts that are close to being competitive but give one party the edge in an election. For instance, if the Democrats control the redistricting process they are likely to draw districts that lean toward the Democratic candidate—55 percent Democrat, 45 percent Republican. Although map makers need to be careful not to draw these too competitive as small swings in the vote could then reverse these districts and instead of a Gerrymander you end with what Grofman and Brunell (2005) call a Dummymander.

25  Poole, Keith and Howard Rosenthal. 1991. "On Dimensionalizing Roll Call Votes in the U.S. Congress." *American Political Science Review* 85(4): 955–960.

26  For instance if a district is 45 percent Republican, 45 percent Democratic and 10 percent Independent, the only votes that matter are those from the smallest group. These independents will only be able to choose from either a Democrat or a Republican in the election, but nonetheless, they become the votes that really count.

27  Proposition 206, passed by Arizona voters in 2000, requires: "To the extent practicable, competitive districts should be favored where to do so would create no significant detriment to the other goals" (sec. 14, subsection F).

28  I highly suggest reading the exchange between Issacharoff (2002) and Persily (2002) on the topic of the utility of competition in congressional elections. As both are also law professors, they also touch on legal issues and the proper role of courts in regulating elections.

29  In fact competitive districts are optimal in this sense.

30  Fiorina, Morris P. 2006. *Culture War? The Myth of a Polarized America.* 2nd edition. New York: Pearson Longman.

31  Ibid., page 214.
32  Ibid., page 217.
33  Huntington, 1950 "A Revised Theory."
34  Fiorina, 1977, *Representatives, Roll Calls.*

## 4 Traditional redistricting principles

1  Of course this statement ignores both the possibility of legislatures overriding a gubernatorial veto, as well as the fact that Nebraska has a unicameral state legislature.
2  Garrett, Elizabeth. 2005. "Redistricting: Another California Revolution?" IRI report, University of Southern California. Online: www.iandrinstitute.org/ REPORT%202005-1%20Redistricting.pdf.
3  At the time of passage there were size states using at-large methods of electing representatives: Alabama, Georgia, Mississippi, Missouri, New Hampshire, New Jersey, Rhode Island all elected from a single statewide district, while Pennsylvania used some single-member districts and some multi-member districts (see Dubin 1998).
4  For an excellent history of the use of single-member districts in America see "A History of One-Winner Districts for Congress" by Nicolas Flores (1999). Available online: www.fairvote.org/library/history/flores/index.html.
5  Gunier, Lani. 1993. "Groups, Representation, and Race-Conscious Districting: A Case of the Emperor's Clothes." *Texas Law Review* 71: 1589.
6  McKay, Robert B. 1963. "Political Thickets and Crazy Quilts." *Michigan Law Review*, 61: 645.
7  Frances E. Lee and Bruce I. Oppenheimer. 1999. *Sizing up the Senate.* Chicago: University of Chicago Press.
8  The Democrats, not surprisingly, continued to litigate the Pennsylvania plan and the new map was appealed to the Supreme Court on the basis of partisan gerrymandering (*Vieth v. Jubuleier*).
9  There is a significant literature on the science of counting people and there has been an on-going discussion in America as to how best to solve the problem of what is called the "differential undercount." The ease of counting people is correlated to certain variables such as income, race, etc. Black people are missed at higher rates than white people for instance. American Indians living on reservations have traditionally been the single group with this largest estimated undercount. For a sampling of this debate see Brunell 2000a, 2000b, 2000c as well as Anderson and Fienberg 2000a and 2000b.
10  See "Should Tiny Deviations from 'One Person, One Vote' be Struck Down?" by Grant Hayden (http://writ.news.findlaw.com/commentary/ 20020827_hayden.html).
11  Quoted in "A Glance at Georgia Redistricting Ruling" by the Associated Press wire, February 10, 2004.
12  Hebert, J. Gerald, Donald B. Verrilli, Jr., Paul M. Smith, Sam Hirsch, and Heather Gerken. 2000. *The Realists' Guide to Redistricting.* Chicago: American Bar Association, page 26.
13  Young, H. Peyton. 1988. "Measuring the Compactness of Legislative Districts." *Legislative Studies Quarterly* 13(1): 105–115. As well as Niemi, Richard G., Bernard Grofman, Carl Carlucci, and Thomas Hofeller. 1990. "Measuring Compactness and the Role of a Compactness Standard in a Test for Partisan and Racial Gerrymandering." *The Journal of Politics* 52(4): 1155–1181.
14  Ernest C. Reock, Jr. 1961. "A Note: Measuring Compactness as a Requirement

of Legislative Apportionment." *Midwest Journal of Political Science* 5(1): 70–74.

15 Ibid., page 71.

16 Young 1988, page 105.

17 I was involved as an expert witness in the first round of redistricting in Texas in 2001. While on the witness stand answering questions about the map that I was hired to evaluate, a lawyer representing a competing map was trying to convince me that his map drew districts to match to some degree what the districts looked like in eastern Texas from the 1950s! Why in the world anyone would want to draw districts the way they looked 50 years ago was beyond me, particularly in a state such as Texas that has changed so much. But the point is clear—communities of interest are not well defined.

18 Butler, David and Bruce E. Cain. 1992. *Congressional Redistricting: Comparative and Theoretical Perspectives*. New York: Macmillan.

19 There is a long-standing debate as to whether *Gingles* is really about "opportunities" or "outcomes," which is to say are we really talking about giving minority voters some chance of controlling the election outcome or does it mean that the outcome itself is what matters, not just the chance to control the outcome. Also for a very nice primer about the legal parameters for redistricting see Hebert et al. 2000. I relied on it heavily for this section of the chapter.

20 www.senate.gov/reference/resources/pdf/RL30378.pdf.

21 www.loc.gov/rr/hispanic/congress/chron.html.

22 Lublin, David, Thomas Brunell, Bernard Grofman, and Lisa Handley. 2007. "Do We Still Need the VRA: In a Word 'YES.' " (January 8). *Center for the Study of Democracy*. Paper 07–02. http://repositories.cdlib.org/csd/07–02.

23 See Susan A. Banducci and Jeffrey A. Karp. 1994. "Electoral Consequences of Scandal and Redistricting in the 1992 House Election." *American Politics Quarterly* 22(1): 3–26.

Kimball Brace, Bernard Grofman, and Lisa Handley. 1987. "Does Redistricting Aimed to Help Black Necessarily Help Republicans?" *The Journal of Politics* 49(1): 143–156.

Hill, Kevin A. 1995. "Does the Creation of Majority Black Districts Aid Representation? An Analysis of the 1992 Congressional Elections in Eight Southern States." *Journal of Politics* 57(2) 384–401.

Lublin, David. 1999. *The Paradox of Representation: Racial Gerrymandering and Minority Interests in Congress*. Princeton: Princeton University Press.

24 Petrocik, John R. and Scott W. Desposato. 1998. "The Partisan Consequences of Majority-Minority Redistricting in the South, 1992 and 1994." *The Journal of Politics* 60(3): 613–633.

## 5 Why competitive elections are bad and noncompetitive elections are good

1 Anderson Christopher J., André Blais, Shaun Bowler, Todd Donovan, and Ola Listhaug. 2005. *Losers' Consent: Elections and Democratic Legitimacy*. Oxford: Oxford University Press, page 186.

2 Nicholas R. Miller. 1983. "Pluralism and Social Choice." *American Political Science Review* 77: 734–747, page 743.

3 It is ironic that my proposal is often criticized because there will be voters who end up on the losing side. "What about those poor people who are in the minority in the district," people say. My response is "sure there will be 20–30 percent who are on the losing side, but that is better than 40–50 percent." I am

explicitly trying to reduce the number of losers and yet I get criticized when there are still some people on the losing side.

4  Fenno, Richard F. 1978. *Home Style: House Members in Their Districts.* Boston: Little, Brown.
   Mayhew, David R. 1974. *Congress: The Electoral Connection.* New Haven: Yale University Press.
5  Technically in House elections one only needs to win a plurality or receive more votes than anyone else, but we can assume that there are only two candidates in an election and one person or the other will receive a majority.
6  Fiorina, Morris P. 1974. *Representatives, Roll Calls, and Constituencies.* Lexington MA: Lexington Books.
7  Huntington, Samuel. 1950. "A Revised Theory of American Party Parties." *American Political Science Review* 44(3): 669–677.
8  Downs, Anthony. 1957. *An Economic Theory of Democracy.* New York: Harper and Row.
9  Buchler, Justin. 2005. "Competition, Representation, and Redistricting: The Case Against Competitive Congressional Districts." *Journal of Theoretical Politics* 17 (4): 431–463. Quote on page 457.
10 Ibid., page 457.
11 McCrone, Donald J., and James H. Kuklinski. 1979. "The Delegate Theory of Representation." *American Journal of Political Science* 23(2): 278–300. Quote on page 278.
12 Miller, Warren E., and Donald E. Stokes. 1963. "Constituency Influence in Congress." *American Political Science Review* 57(1): 45–56.
13 Ibid., page 56.
14 See Robert S. Erikson, Norman R. Luttbeg, and William V. Holloway. 1975. "Knowing One's District: How Legislator's Predict Referendum Voting." *American Journal of Political Science* 19(2): 231–246.
   Erikson, Robert. 1978. "Constituency Opinion and Congressional Behavior: A Reexamination of the Miller-Stokes Data." *American Journal of Political Science* 22(3): 511–535.
15 Justice O'Connor and Justice Rehnquist wrote a separate opinion in this case that foreshadowed their thinking nearly 20 years later in the *Vieth v. Pennsylvania* case—they felt that the question is nonjusticiable in large part because no manageable standards could be derived to indicate when a plan constitutes a gerrymander.
16 Issacharoff, Samuel. 1993. "Judging Politics: The Elusive Quest for Judicial Review of Political Fairness." *Texas Law Review.* 71: 1643–1671.
17 Grofman, Bernard. 1992. "An Expert Witness Perspective on Continuing and Emerging Voting Rights Controversies." *Stetson Law Review* 21: 783–816.
18 Issacharoff, Samuel, Pamela S. Karlan, and Richard H. Pildes. 2002. *The Law of Democracy: Legal Structure of the Political Process.* 2nd revised edition. Westbury, New York: Foundation Press, page 886.
19 Dahl, Robert A. 1998. *On Democracy.* New Haven: Yale University Press.
20 Ibid., page 134.
21 We do not see this happen very often in American elections since most of the time there are only two credible candidates for office. Far more likely, we actually see uncontested general elections with the single major party candidate receiving all the votes.
22 Brady, Henry E., Michael C. Herron, Walter R. Mebane Jr., Jasjeet Singh

Sekhon, Kenneth W. Shotts, and Jonathan Wand. 2001. "Law and Data: The Butterfly Ballot Episode" *PS: Political Science and Politics* 34(1): 59–69.

Wand, Jonathan N., Kenneth W. Shotts, Jasjeet S. Sekhon, Walter R. Mebane, Jr., Michael C. Herron, Henry E. Brady. 2001. "The Butterfly Did It: The Aberrant Vote for Buchanan in Palm Beach County, Florida." *American Political Science Review* 95(4): 793–810.

23 In this example I am accusing the Democrats of being undemocratic, but make no mistake, if the Republicans faced the same situation, they would act in a similar fashion. Both parties want to win elections and if they have avenues of recourse available to them to increase their chances of winning, they will explore all of these avenues.

24 Ibid.

25 Buchler, Justin. 2007. "The Statistical Properties of Competitive Districts: What the Central Limit Theorem Can Teach Us about Election Reform." *PS: Political Science and Politics* 40(2): 333–337.


## 6 Addressing the critiques

1 "Redistricting Defeats," *Washington Post*, November 14, 2005, page A20.

2 The above causal logic is borrowed from Grofman and Brunell (2005b).

3 See Brunell and Grofman (2008).

4 Ono, Keiko. 2005. "Electoral Origins of Partisan Polarization in Congress: Debunking the Myth." *Extensions* (Carl Albert Research Center) Fall: 15–19. Quote on page 19.

5 See Grofman and Brunell (2008).

6 Theriault, Sean. 2005. "Redistricting and Party Polarization in Congress." Paper prepared for presentation at the American Political Science Association Annual Meeting, Washington, DC, September 1–4, 2005.

7 This general trend is true using a wide variety of ideological scores from many different interest groups, see Lee, Moretti, and Butler 2004.

8 Ansolabehere, Stephen, James Snyder, and Charles Stewart. 2001. "Candidate Positioning in U.S. House Elections." *American Journal of Political Science* 45: 136–59.

9 Issacharoff, Samuel, Burt Neuborne, and Richard H. Pildes. 2006. Amicus brief filed in the *Jackson v. Perry* case, page 11.

10 Lott, John R., Jr. and Stephen G. Bronars. 1993. "Time Series Evidence on Shirking in the U.S. House of Representatives." *Public Choice* 74: 461–484.

Poole, Keith T. and Thomas Romer. 1993. "Ideology, 'Shirking,' and Representation." *Public Choice* 77: 185–196.

Poole, Keith T. 1998. "Changing Minds? Not in Congress!" *GSIA Working Paper #1997–22.* Carnegie-Mellon University.

Poole, Keith, and Howard Rosenthal. 1997. *Congress: A Political-Economic History of Roll-Call Voting.* New York: Oxford University Press.

11 Rothenberg, Lawrence S. and Mitchell S. Sanders. 2000. "Severing the Electoral Connection: Shirking in the Contemporary Congress." *American Journal of Political Science* 44: 316–325.

12 Carson, Jamie L., Michael H. Crespin, Jeffrey Jenkins, and Ryan J. Vander Wielen. 2004. "Shirking in the Contemporary Congress: A Reappraisal." *Political Analysis* 12: 176–179.

13 Fenno, Richard F. 1978. *Home Style: House Members in Their Districts.* Boston: Little, Brown, page 10.

14 Cleary, Matthew R. 2007. "Electoral Competition, Participation, and Government Responsiveness in Mexico." *American Journal of Political Science* 51(2): 283–299. Quote on page 297.

15 Mayhew, David R. 1974. *Congress: The Electoral Connection.* New Haven: Yale University Press, page 37.

16 In the 2000 House elections, 398 incumbents ran for reelection and only six lost—or about 1.5 percent.

17 President Bush carried this district by a larger margin than in any other district in Illinois.

18 Hanks, Christopher and Bernard Grofman. 1998. "Turnout in Gubernatorial and Senatorial Primary and General Elections in the South, 1922–90: A Rational Choice Model of the Effects of Short-run and Long-run Electoral Competition on Relative Turnout." *Public Choice* 94(3–4): 407–421.

19 Jewell, Malcolm E. and Lee Sigelman. 1986. "Voting in Primaries: The Impact of Intra- and Inter-Party Competition." *The Western Political Quarterly* 39(3): 446–454. Quote on page 453.

20 Kenny, Patrick J. 1988. "Sorting Out the Effects of Primary Divisiveness in Congressional and Senatorial Elections." *The Western Political Quarterly* 41(4): 765–777.
   Born, Richard. 1981. "The Influence of House Primary Election Divisiveness on General Election Margins 1962–1976." *Journal of Politics* 42: 640–666.

21 Quoted in J. Hoeffel, "Six Incumbents Are a Week Away from Easy Election," *Winston-Salem Jo*urnal, Jan. 27, 1998, page B1.

22 Laakso, M. and R. Taagepera. 1979. "Effective Number of Parties: A Measure with Application to West Europe." *Comparative Political Studies* 12: 3–27.

23 A simple way to think about the swing ratio is that it is the slope of the seats votes curve.

24 Most PR systems do use a "threshold" percentage, below which a party will not get any seats in parliament. Typically these thresholds range from 3–5 percent of the vote.

25 Most PR systems have a swing ratio of roughly 1, but it is typically not *exactly* equal to 1 because these electoral systems usually create a threshold (say 5 percent for instance), which means that the very smallest parties, those with vote share below the threshold, receive no seats in the legislature.

26 This should make sense if you think about the Democrats winning 80 percent of the vote nationwide for all House elections, Republicans are not going to be winning very many seats.

27 Gelman, Andrew and Gary King. 1994a. "Enhancing Democracy Through Legislative Redistricting." *The American Political Science Review* 88(3): 541–559. See page 544.

28 If possible, I think it is preferable to draw all districts in a packed manner, but this may not be possible in every state.

29 www.britannica.com/presidents/article-9116853.

30 Arend Lijphart. 1995. *Electoral Systems and Party Systems A Study of Twenty-Seven Democracies, 1945–1990.* Oxford: Oxford University Press.

31 Bernard Grofman and Gary King. 2007. "The Future of Partisan Symmetry as a Judicial Test for Partisan Gerrymandering after LULAC v. Perry." *Election Law Journal* 6(1): 2–35.

32 Wattenberg, Martin P. 1998. *The Decline of American Political Parties, 1952–1996.* Cambridge, MA: Harvard University Press.

33 Fiorina, Morris P. 2006. *Culture War? The Myth of a Polarized America.* 2nd edition. New York: Pearson Longman, page 218.

34 Keith, Bruce E., David B. Magleby, Candice J. Nelson, Elizabeth Orr, Mark C. Westlye, and Raymond E. Wolfinger. 1992. *The Myth of the Independent Voter*. Berkeley, CA: University of California Press.

35 Roughly half the states use some form of a closed primary to nominate candidates, while the other half use some form of an open primary (See Grofman and Brunell 2001).

36 Anderson Christopher J., André Blais, Shaun Bowler, Todd Donovan, and Ola Listhaug. 2005. *Losers' Consent: Elections and Democratic Legitimacy*. Oxford: Oxford University Press.

37 This is true regardless of who draws the maps. Some states give the power to redraw district lines to "nonpartisan" commissions rather than having the state legislature and the governor, while it is not clear that we could expect more from an independent commission than from the state government, it matters not if all districts are packed. Assuming that both parties are packed to the same degree on average across the state, gerrymandering is simply not possible.

## 7 Conclusion

1 Stephanopoulos, Nicholas. 2007. "Reforming Redistricting: Why Popular Initiatives to Establish Redistricting Commissions Succeed or Fail." Issue Brief of the American Constitution Society for Law and Policy. Online: www.acslaw.org/node/4414.

2 Ibid.

3 Donald Stokes in the 1980s and 1990s and Larry Bartels in the 2000 round.

4 I am by no means criticizing the job that professors Stokes and Bartels did, nor do I think that either one of them was overly partisan. The fact of the matter is that as an appointee to an ad hoc committee, we rely on a sense of duty to keep this person in line. I simply prefer elections to keep people responsive.

5 Cox, Adam B. 2006. "Designing Redistricting Institutions." Public Law and Legal Theory Working Paper #131, University of Chicago Law School

6 Although the recent Supreme Court decision for the Texas redistricting case has left the door open for more mid-decade redistricting, the Court refused to put a stop to partisan gerrymandering.

7 Hayes, Brian. 1996. "Computing Science: Machine Politics." *American Scientist* 84(6): 522–526.

8 Ibid.

9 All of these are from "Democracy in a Noose," by David Lebedoff, the *Washington Post*, April 7, 2001, A19.

10 "REDISTRICTING: Disenfranchised Voters Can Defeat Manipulators at Polls," by Jim Wooten, *The Atlanta Journal-Constitution*, August 3, 2001, A 18.

11 Fiorina, Morris P. 2006. *Culture War? The Myth of a Polarized America*. 2nd edition. New York: Pearson Longman, footnote 55 on page 218. See also chapters 8 and 10 in McDonald and Samples (2006) for further discussion.

12 Gerrymander. Dictionary.com. *The American Heritage Dictionary of the English Language, Fourth Edition*. Houghton Mifflin Company, 2004. http://dictionary.reference.com/browse/gerrymander (accessed: June 14, 2007).

# References

Anderson, Christopher J. and Christine A. Guillory. 1997. "Political Institutions and Satisfaction with Democracy: A Cross-National Analysis of Consensus and Majoritarian Systems." *American Political Science Review* 91(1): 66–81.

Anderson, Christopher J. and Andrew J. LoTempio. 2002. "Winning, Losing, and Political Trust in America." *British Journal of Political Science* 32: 335–351.

Anderson Christopher J., André Blais, Shaun Bowler, Todd Donovan, and Ola Listhaug. 2005. *Losers' Consent: Elections and Democratic Legitimacy.* Oxford: Oxford University Press.

Anderson, Margo and Stephen E. Fienberg. 2000a. "History, Myth Making, and Statistics: A Short Story about the Reapportionment of Congress and the 1990 Census." *PS: Political Science & Politics.* 33(4): 783–792.

Anderson, Margo and Stephen E. Fienberg. 2000b. "Partisan Politics at Work: Sampling and the 2000 Census," *PS: Political Science & Politics.* 33(4): 795–800.

Ansolabehere, Stephen, James Snyder, and Charles Stewart. 2001. "Candidate Positioning in U.S. House Elections." *American Journal of Political Science* 45: 136–159.

Banducci, Susan A. and Jeffrey A. Karp. 1994. "Electoral Consequences of Scandal and Redistricting in the 1992 House Election." *American Politics Quarterly* 22(1): 3–26.

Barreto, Matt. and Streb, Matthew. 2007. "Barn Burners and Burn Out: The Effects of Competitive Elections on Efficacy and Trust." Paper presented at the annual meeting of the Midwest Political Science Association.

Born, Richard. 1981. "The Influence of House Primary Election Divisiveness on General Election Margins 1962–1976." *Journal of Politics* 42: 640–661.

Bowler, Shaun and Todd Donovan. 2002. "Democracy, Institutions and Attitudes about Citizen Influence on Government." *British Journal of Political Science* 32(4): 371–390.

Brace, Kimball, Bernard Grofman, and Lisa Handley. 1987. "Does Redistricting Aimed to Help Blacks Necessarily Help Republicans?" *The Journal of Politics* 49(1): 143–156.

Brady, Henry E., Michael C. Herron, Walter R. Mebane Jr., Jasjeet Singh Sekhon, Kenneth W. Shotts, and Jonathan Wand. 2001. "Law and Data: The Butterfly Ballot Episode." *PS: Political Science and Politics* 34(1): 59–69.

Brunell, Thomas L. 2000a. "Using Statistical Sampling to Estimate the U.S. Population: The Political and Methodological Debate over Census 2000." *PS: Political Science and Politics.* 33(4): 775–782.

Brunell, Thomas L. 2000b. "Rejoinder to Anderson and Fienberg." *PS: Political Science and Politics.* 33(4): 793–794.

Brunell, Thomas L. 2000c. "Making Sense of the Census: It's Political." *PS: Political Science and Politics.* 33(4, December): 801–802.

Brunell, Thomas L. 2006. "Rethinking Redistricting: How Drawing Uncompetitive Districts Eliminates Gerrymanders, Enhances Representation, and Improves Attitudes Toward Congress." *PS: Political Science & Politics,* 39(1) 77–86.

Brunell, Thomas L. and Justin Buchler. 2007. "Ideological Representation and Competitive Congressional Districts: Some Empirical Observations." Typescript, University of Texas at Dallas.

Brunell, Thomas L. and Bernard Grofman, 2008. "Evaluating the Impact of Redistricting on District Homogeneity, Political Competition, and Political Extremism in the U.S. House of Representatives, 1962–2002." In *"Mobilizing Democracy: A Comparative Perspective on Institutional Barriers and Political Obstacles,"* Margaret Levi, James Johnson, Jack Knight, and Susan Stokes, editors. New York: Russell Sage Press.

Buchler, Justin. 2005. "Competition, Representation, and Redistricting: The Case Against Competitive Congressional Districts." *Journal of Theoretical Politics* 17(4): 431–463.

Buchler, Justin. 2007. "The Statistical Properties of Competitive Districts: What the Central Limit Theorem Can Teach Us about Election Reform." *PS: Political Science and Politics* 40(2): 333–337.

Butler, David and Bruce E. Cain. 1992. *Congressional Redistricting: Comparative and Theoretical Perspectives.* New York: Macmillan.

Carson, Jamie L., Michael H. Crespin, Jeffrey Jenkins, and Ryan J. Vander Wielen. 2004. "Shirking in the Contemporary Congress: A Reappraisal." *Political Analysis* 12: 176–179.

Clarke, Harold D. and Alan C. Acock. 1989. "National Elections and Political Attitudes: The Case of Political Efficacy." *British Journal of Political Science* 19(4): 551–562.

Clarke, Harold D. and Allan Kornberg. 1992. "Do National Elections Affect Perceptions of MP Responsiveness? A Note on the Canadian Case." *Legislative Studies Quarterly* 17(2): 183–204.

Cleary, Matthew R. 2007. "Electoral Competition, Participation, and Government Responsiveness in Mexico." *American Journal of Political Science* 51(2): 283–299.

Cox, Adam B. 2006. "Designing Redistricting Institutions." Public Law and Legal Theory Working Paper #131, University of Chicago Law School.

Cox, Gary W. and Jonathan N. Katz. 2002. *Elbridge Gerry's Salamander: The Electoral Consequences of the Reapportionment Revolution.* Cambridge: Cambridge University Press.

Dahl, Robert A. 1956. *A Preface to Democratic Theory.* Chicago: University of Chicago Press.

Downs, Anthony. 1957. *An Economic Theory of Democracy.* New York: Harper and Row.

Dubin, Michael J. 1998. *United States Congressional Elections, 1788–1997.* London: McFarland and Company.

Erikson, Robert S., Norman R. Luttbeg, and William V. Holloway. 1975. "Knowing One's District: How Legislator's Predict Referendum Voting." *American Journal of Political Science* 19(2): 231–246.

Eulau, Heinz and Paul D. Karps. 1977. "The Puzzle of Representation: Specifying Components of Responsiveness." *Legislative Studies Quarterly* 2(3): 233–254.

Fenno, Richard F. 1978. *Home Style: House Members in Their Districts.* Boston: Little, Brown.

Fiorina, Morris P. 1974. *Representatives, Roll Calls, and Constituencies.* Lexington MA: Lexington Books.

Fiorina, Morris P. 2006. *Culture War? The Myth of a Polarized America.* 2nd edition. New York: Pearson Longman.

Garrett, Elizabeth. 2005. "Redistricting: Another California Revolution?" IRI report, University of Southern California. Online: www.iandrinstitute.org/REPORT%202005–1%20Redistricting.pdf.

Gelman, Andrew and Gary King. 1994a. "Enhancing Democracy Through Legislative Redistricting." *The American Political Science Review* 88(3): 541–559.

Granberg, Donald and Edward Brent. 1983. "When Prophecy Bends: The Preference-expectation Link in U.S. Presidential Elections, 1952–1980." *Journal of Personality and Social Psychology* 45: 477–491.

Grofman, Bernard. 1992. "An Expert Witness Perspective on Continuing and Emerging Voting Rights Controversies." *Stetson Law Review* 21: 783–816.

Grofman, Bernard and Thomas L. Brunell. 2001. "Explaining the Ideological Differences Between the Two U.S. Senators Elected from the Same State: An Institutional Effects Model," in *Congressional Primaries and the Politics of Representation.* Eds Peter F. Galderisi, Marni Ezra, and Michael Lyons. Boston: Rowman and Littlefield.

Grofman, Bernard and Thomas L. Brunell. 2005. "The Art of the Dummymander: The Impact of Recent Redistrictings on the Partisan Makeup of Southern House Seats," in *Redistricting in the New Millennium.* Ed. Peter Galderisi. New York: Lexington Books.

Grofman, Bernard and Gary King. 2007. "The Future of Partisan Symmetry as a Judicial Test for Partisan Gerrymandering after LULAC v. Perry." *Election Law Journal* 6(1): 2–35.

Guinier, Lani. 1993. "Groups, Representation, and Race-Conscious Districting: A Case of the Emperor's Clothes." *Texas Law Review* 71: 1589.

Guinier, Lani. 1994. *The Tyranny of the Majority: Fundamental Fairness in Representative Democracy.* New York: Free Press.

Hanks, Christopher and Bernard Grofman. 1998. "Turnout in Gubernatorial and Senatorial Primary and General Elections in the South, 1922–90: A Rational Choice Model of the Effects of Short-run and Long-run Electoral Competition on Relative Turnout." *Public Choice* 94(3–4): 407–421.

Hayes, Brian. 1996. "Computing Science: Machine Politics." *American Scientist* 84(6): 522–526.

Hebert, J. Gerald, Donald B. Verrilli, Jr., Paul M. Smith, Sam Hirsch, and Heather Gerken. 2000. *The Realists' Guide to Redistricting.* Chicago: American Bar Association.

Hibbing, John R. and Elizabeth Theiss-Morse. 1995. *Congress as Public Enemy: Public Attitudes towards American Political Institutions.* Cambridge: Cambridge University Press.

Hibbing, John R. and James T. Smith. 2001. "What the American Public Wants Congress to Be," in *Congress Reconsidered.* 7th edition. Eds Lawrence C. Dodd and Bruce I. Oppenheimer. Washington DC: CQ Press.

Hill, Kevin A. 1995. "Does the Creation of Majority Black Districts Aid Representation? An Analysis of the 1992 Congressional Elections in Eight Southern States." *Journal of Politics* 57(2): 384–401.

Hirsch, Sam. 2003. "The United States House of Unrepresentatives: What Went Wrong in the Latest Round of Congressional Redistricting." *Election Law Journal* 2(2): 179–216.

Huntington, Samuel. 1950. "A Revised Theory of American Party Parties." *American Political Science Review* 44(3): 669–677.

Issacharoff, Samuel. 1993. "Judging Politics: The Elusive Quest for Judicial Review of Political Fairness." *Texas Law Review* 71: 1643–1671.

Issacharoff, Samuel. 2002. "Gerrymandering and Political Cartels." *Harvard Law Review* (116): 593–648.

Issacharoff, Samuel, Pamela S. Karlan, and Richard H. Pildes. 2002. *The Law of Democracy: Legal Structure of the Political Process.* 2nd revised edition. Westbury, New York: Foundation Press.

Issacharoff, Samuel, Burt Neuborne, and Richard H. Pildes. 2006. Amicus brief filed in the *Jackson v. Perry* case.

Jewell, Malcolm E. and Lee Sigelman. 1986. "Voting in Primaries: The Impact of Intra- and Inter-Party Competition." *The Western Political Quarterly* 39(3): 446–454.

Keith, Bruce E., David B. Magleby, Candice J. Nelson, Elizabeth Orr, Mark C. Westlye, and Raymond E. Wolfinger. 1992. *The Myth of the Independent Voter.* Berkeley, CA: University of California Press.

Kenny, Patrick J. 1988. "Sorting Out the Effects of Primary Divisiveness in Congressional and Senatorial Elections." *The Western Political Quarterly* 41(4): 765–777.

Koetzle, William. 1998. "The Impact of Constituency Diversity upon the Competitiveness of U.S. House of Representatives Elections, 1962–1996." *Legislative Studies Quarterly* 23: 561–574.

Laakso, M. and R. Taagepera. 1979. "Effective Number of Parties: A Measure with Application to West Europe." *Comparative Political Studies* (12): 3–27.

Lee, David S., Enrico Moretti, and Matthew J. Butler. 2004. "Do Voters Affect or Elect Policies? Evidence from the U.S. House." *Quarterly Journal of Economics* 1993(3): 807–859.

Lee, Frances E. and Bruce I. Oppenheimer. 1999. *Sizing up the Senate.* Chicago: University of Chicago Press.

Lijphart, Arend. 1995. *Electoral Systems and Party Systems: A Study of Twenty-Seven Democracies, 1945–1990.* Oxford: Oxford University Press.

Lott, John R., Jr. and Stephen G. Bronars. 1993. "Time Series Evidence on Shirking in the U.S. House of Representatives." *Public Choice* 74: 461–484.

Lublin, David. 1999. *The Paradox of Representation: Racial Gerrymandering and Minority Interests in Congress.* Princeton: Princeton University Press.

Lublin, David, Thomas Brunell, Bernard Grofman, and Lisa Handley. 2007. "Do We Still Need the VRA: In a Word 'YES.' " (January 8). *Center for the Study of Democracy*. Paper 07–02. http://repositories.cdlib.org/csd/07–02.

Manin, Bernard. 1997. *The Principles of Representative Government*. Cambridge: Cambridge University Press.

Mann, Thomas E. and Bruce E. Cain. 2005. "Introduction," in *Party Lines*. Eds Thomas E. Mann and Bruce E. Cain. Washington DC: Brooking Press.

Mayhew, David R. 1974. *Congress: The Electoral Connection*. New Haven: Yale University Press.

McCrone, Donald J. and James H. Kuklinski. 1979. "The Delegate Theory of Representation." *American Journal of Political Science* 23(2): 278–300.

McDonald, Michael P. and John Samples, eds. 2006. *The Marketplace Of Democracy: Electoral Competition and American Politics*. Washington DC: Brookings Institute.

McKay, Robert B. 1963. "Political Thickets and Crazy Quilts." *Michigan Law Review* 61: 645.

Miller, Nicholas R. 1983. "Pluralism and Social Choice." *American Political Science Review* 77: 734–747.

Miller, Warren E. and Donald E. Stokes. 1963. "Constituency Influence in Congress." *American Political Science Review* 57(1): 45–56.

Niemi, Richard G., Bernard Grofman, Carl Carlucci, and Thomas Hofeller. 1990. "Measuring Compactness and the Role of a Compactness Standard in a Test for Partisan and Racial Gerrymandering." *The Journal of Politics* 52(4): 1155–1181.

Ono, Keiko. 2005. "Electoral Origins of Partisan Polarization in Congress: Debunking the Myth." *Extensions* (Carl Albert Research Center) Fall: 15–19.

Persily, Nathan. 2002. "In Defense of Foxes Guarding Henhouses: The Case for Judicial Acquiescence to Incumbent Protecting Gerrymanders." *Harvard Law Review* (116): 649–683.

Petrocik, John R. and Scott W. Desposato. 1998. "The Partisan Consequences of Majority-Minority Redistricting in the South, 1992 and 1994." *The Journal of Politics* 60(3): 613–633.

Pitkin, Hannah F. 1967. *The Concept of Representation*. Berkeley: University of California Press.

Poole, Keith T. 1998. "Changing Minds? Not in Congress!" *GSIA Working Paper #1997–22*. Carnegie-Mellon University.

Poole, Keith T. and Thomas Romer. 1993. "Ideology, 'Shirking,' and Representation." *Public Choice* 77: 185–196.

Poole, Keith and Howard Rosenthal. 1991. "On Dimensionalizing Roll Call Votes in the U.S. Congress." *American Political Science Review* 85(4): 955–960.

Regan, Dennis T. and Martin Kilduff. 1988. "Optimism about Elections: Dissonance Reduction at the Ballot Box." *Political Psychology* 9(1): 101–107.

Rehfeld, Andrew. 2005. *The Concept of Constituency: Political Representation, Democratic Legitimacy and Institutional Design*. Cambridge: Cambridge University Press.

Reock, Ernest C., Jr. 1961. "A Note: Measuring Compactness as a Requirement of Legislative Apportionment." *Midwest Journal of Political Science* 5(1): 70–74.

Rothenberg, Lawrence S. and Mitchell S. Sanders. 2000. "Severing the Electoral Connection: Shirking in the Contemporary Congress." *American Journal of Political Science* 44: 316–325.

Schumpeter, Joseph. 1942. *Capitalism, Socialism, and Democracy.* New York: Harper and Row.

Stephanopoulos, Nicholas. 2007. "Reforming Redistricting: Why Popular Initiatives to Establish Redistricting Commissions Succeed or Fail." Issue Brief of the American Constitution Society for Law and Policy. Online: www.acslaw.org/node/4414.

Theriault, Sean. 2005. "Redistricting and Party Polarization in Congress." Paper prepared for presentation at the American Political Science Association Annual Meeting, Washington, DC, September 1–4, 2005.

Verba, Sidney and Norman H. Nie. 1972. *Participation in America: Political Democracy and Social Equality.* New York: Harper and Row.

Wand, Jonathan N., Kenneth W. Shotts, Jasjeet S. Sekhon, Walter R. Mebane, Jr., Michael C. Herron, and Henry E. Brady. 2001. "The Butterfly Did It: The Aberrant Vote for Buchanan in Palm Beach County, Florida." *American Political Science Review* 95(4): 793–810.

Wattenberg, Martin P. 1998. *The Decline of American Political Parties, 1952–1996.* Cambridge, MA: Harvard University Press.

Young, H. Peyton. 1988. "Measuring the Compactness of Legislative Districts." *Legislative Studies Quarterly* 13(1): 105–115.

# Index